U.S. Voti   ...arency

U.S. Voting Trar
reliable way for an and ...
and have their votes counted correctly.

Eliminating doubts about voting results, will
eliminate doubts about whether we live in a
democracy.

Federal and state voting needs to be done by
citizens using their online account at
socialsecurity.gov where citizens can update
things like their legal name and address. SSA
(Social Security Administration) and the states
would jointly determine who is eligible to vote
based on all federal and state information. A
unique number would be assigned to each
person's vote and would be on both the vote
copy that remains in the online account and the
vote copy that immediately goes to the state
without the voter's name.

Each voter would be able to go to their online
account and see their vote as counted in the SSA
voting results. There should be no differences
between SSA voting results and each state's
voting results.

John J. Rodenkirch, CPA, CMA, CFM, CGMA

This book's financial forecasts, projections, statements, and opinions concerning things like an economic crisis/crash, interest rates, inflation rates, investing, and the stock market are just possibilities. Author, editor, and publisher do not claim any competency concerning matters in this book. Readers should consult with competent professionals before taking any actions concerning anything in this book.

Author can be contacted at:
John@USvotingtransparency.org

ISBN: 978-1-7344210-1-9

EP - Explanation Press

Seminole, FL

Dedication

This book is dedicated to everyone who believes that all Men and Women have certain unalienable Rights that among these are Life, Liberty, and the Pursuit of Happiness. That to secure these Rights, Governments are instituted among Men and Women, deriving their just Powers from the Consent of the Governed.

Contents

Contents

Introduction

U.S. Voting Transparency fixes the root problems with our voting system. Congress' For the People Act of 2021 just makes the root problems worse.

U.S. Voting Transparency is needed for:
- federal and state primaries
- federal and state elections
- state ballot initiatives and referendums, especially those that concern economic efficiency
- ratification of U.S. Constitutional Amendments
- use when federal government spending soon crashes our economy
- opinion surveys, so we know what the majority of voters really think
- direct democracy, for when our elected representatives are intimidated by those who use force to achieve political and social goals

The Voting Transparency chapter explains how voters can:
- get Congress to add the voting system at socialsecurity.gov
- get the states to use the voting system

The economic efficiency ideas on the back cover of this book are explained further in the "Economic Efficiency" chapter.

This book also explains the following: The U.S. Constitution was written such that the federal government, the state legislatures, and the people, would each be subject to a check and balance from the other two. The check and balance on the federal government is blocked by the federal government. The Constitution's Article VII Check and Balance enables the state legislatures and the people to reestablish their check and balance on the federal government. The federal government will stop blocking this check and balance when the state legislatures and the people get close to using the Article VII Check and Balance.

Citizens need to limit how much Congress spends, so Congress does not:

- crash both our economy and our societal safety net. Congress' Federal Debt is now over $28 trillion and is growing by over $1 trillion a year. The larger the debt, the worse the crash will be. Spending more than our economy earns, has to be eventually offset by spending less than our economy earns.

 - "rebuild" both our economy and our societal safety net after they crash, without any meaningful input from the people and the state legislatures. States will need protection from things like additional unfunded federal mandates. People will need protection from things like additional federal government control of businesses that will cause increases in business costs and decreases in inflation-adjusted wages.

 - use the "national emergency" caused by the crash, to further reduce our U.S. Constitutional Rights.

The $28 trillion Federal Debt above excludes the following:

 - $10 trillion for Federal Agency Debt (Fannie Mae, Freddie Mac, Ginnie Mae, and Federal Home Loan Banks).

 - money deducted from people's paychecks for Social Security and Medicare, which should have been saved for when they retire and not spent by Congress for things that the Washington-Special-Interest groups wanted. Unfunded liabilities for Social Security and Medicare total $55 trillion.

 - unfunded liabilities for Medicaid of at least $12 trillion.

The Citizens Limit Congress Amendment will:

- enable people and state legislatures to reduce federal government spending

- enable people and state legislatures to redirect federal government spending, with a majority vote of people in each of any three-fourths of the states or by state legislatures in each of any three-fourths of the states, respectively

- enable people to propose U.S. Constitutional Amendments by a majority vote of people in each of any two-thirds of the states that can be fully ratified by state legislatures in each of any three-fourths of the states

- enable state legislatures in each of any two-thirds of the states to propose U.S. Constitutional Amendments that can be fully ratified by a majority vote of people in each of any three-fourths of the states

- restore the Constitution's check and balance on the federal government with changes to the check and balance so that it can never again be blocked by the federal government

 - be the only way we have to limit Congress from crashing then "rebuilding" our economy/societal safety net and then using the "national emergency" caused by the crash, to further reduce our constitutional rights

Enabling people to propose amendments is required to make sure that the people's ideas for amendments are considered.

Enabling people and state legislatures to propose amendments and ratify each other's proposed amendments is critical to protect the people and state legislatures' constitutional rights forever.

All of the above can be established by people and state legislatures, the same way they established the U.S. Constitution. Congress will make this unnecessary by proposing the Citizens Limit Congress Amendment that people and state legislatures get close to establishing without federal government involvement. By doing this, Congress will keep the Article VII Check and Balance unused and make it much less likely to ever be needed.

Only the state legislatures can start the process of using the Article VII check and balance. Ideally, they will have their first joint meeting before the crash.

Our state legislatures need to get working together and agree on a version of the Citizens Limit Congress Amendment for Congress to propose, before the state legislatures are blamed for letting the crash occur.

Enabling people and state legislatures to propose amendments and ratify each other's proposed amendments is critical for the following additional reason.

Our state legislatures and people need to be wary of false promises and Acts from Congress that will supposedly fix federal government spending. Back in the 1980s and 1990s people wanted Congress to balance the budget. Congress responded by passing a bunch of balanced budget type Acts. The people thought they had achieved their goal and moved on to other things. By the time that all these Acts failed to balance the budget, the people had nothing to hold Congress to its promises. Congress used the same scheme when people wanted campaign finance reform. The "Lock-Box" for social security positive cash flows is another example of false promises and Acts from Congress. Congress borrowed the money in the "Lock-Box" and spent it. Projections about when social security will run out of money are based on the "Lock-Box" money being used to pay social security benefits. When people became concerned about the federal government debt, Congress set a limit on the federal government debt. When the actual debt gets close to the limit, Congress has to increase the limit or the government shuts down. When Congress does this, they spend hundreds of billions of dollars more and claim that they had to spend the money in order to keep the government from shutting down.

The federal government cannot be allowed to continue unconstitutionally blocking the Constitution's check and balance on the federal government. See the "Congress Refuses to Call an Article V Convention" and the "Article V of the U.S. Constitution" chapters in this book.

Even if Congress calls an Article V Convention based on applications received in the past, there is not enough time to use the convention to stop

Congress from crashing both our economy and our societal safety net. Even if there is enough time, the Supreme Court's "Political Question" doctrine would enable Congress to cause all kinds of problems with the Article V Convention. Congress' excuse for not calling an Article V Convention for the last 100 years or so is that Congress does not have a procedure for counting the states' applications. Imagine what Alexander Hamilton's response would be to this excuse.

The more power that Congress takes from the people and from the state legislatures, the more money that Washington-special-interest groups will spend helping our federal elected representatives stay in office and prosper. I wonder how much lower Congress' approval rating by the people is than what Congress' approval rating by the Washington-special-interest groups would be. People's approval rating of Congress seems to be a fair measurement of the people's consent of the governed.

When the people established their U.S. Federal Government, they also established the Article V and Article VII checks and balances. This enabled the people, working with their state legislatures, to keep enough control to prevent Congress from doing anything significantly detrimental to the country, like crashing both our economy and societal safety net.

The Article VII Check and Balance is the "two-thirds of the states" Check and Balance that protects the Article V "three-fourths of the states" Check and Balance.

The different groups of state legislatures that want to propose different U.S. Constitutional Amendments, need to first work together. They need to restore the Constitution's check and balance on the federal government with changes to the check and balance so that it can never again be blocked by the federal government. Their current lack of much interest in amendments is because the state legislatures have submitted over 500 valid applications for an Article V Convention and Congress just refuses to call the convention.

These different groups of state legislatures cannot allow themselves to be split up into opposing groups, which is what will be attempted by the federal government, Washington-special-interest groups, and by some news media that advocate for centralized government.

In The Federalist 85, where Alexander Hamilton reaffirms the state legislatures' right to propose amendments, he states, "We may safely rely on the disposition of the State legislatures to erect barriers against the encroachments of the national authority."

The federal government's spending programs have us headed for a financial-market revolt against our Treasury bonds, which will cause the long-term crash of our societal safety net. It would then take decades before our societal safety net grows to the sustainable level it could have been maintained at, if the state legislatures and the people had established the Citizens Limit Congress Amendment and used it to limit federal government spending programs to sustainable levels.

The federal government is unable to limit spending to sustainable levels, because of Washington-special-interest groups that enable our federal elected politicians to stay in office and prosper in return for (1) keeping the spending up and (2) building inefficiencies in our economy that benefit the Washington-special-interest groups.

Each of the two reasons below is more than enough to justify establishing the Citizens Limit Congress Amendment.

1. To preserve our societal safety net at a sustainable level, by reducing federal government spending programs to sustainable levels that will prevent a financial-market revolt against our Treasury bonds from crashing our economy and societal safety net.

2. If the state legislatures and people cannot propose and ratify amendments soon enough, they will need this right permanently restored so they

will have some meaningful input when Congress attempts to "rebuild" our crashed economy and societal safety net. Without this meaningful input, Congress will be unable to stand up to the Washington-special-interest groups that will have already caused Congress to crash our economy and societal safety net. Congress will continue down the same path, increasing federal debt, increasing unfunded federal mandates, building more inefficiencies into both our economy and the regulations that our states are forced to follow, and encroaching further on our Constitutional rights.

Overview:

 - Article V of the U.S. Constitution contains a check and balance that gives the state legislatures the right to propose amendments to the Constitution that the people can ratify.

 - The state legislatures and the people have needed to use the above check and balance for the last 13 years to limit Congress from borrowing an average of a trillion dollars each year since the 2008 Financial Crisis, excluding pandemic spending.

 - The Supreme Court's "Political Question" doctrine, which has no basis in the Constitution, has enabled Congress to block the state legislatures from using the Article V Check and Balance.

 - Article VII of our Constitution contains a check and balance that permanently protects the constitutional right to propose amendments, in a manner that it cannot ever be blocked by the federal government again. Congress will make this unnecessary by proposing the Citizens Limit Congress Amendment that people and state legislatures get close to establishing the same way they established the U.S. Constitution. By doing this, Congress will keep the Article VII Check and Balance unused and make it much less likely to ever be needed.

 - Only the state legislatures can start the process of using the Article VII Check and Balance. Ideally, they will have their first joint meeting before the crash.

Since Article VII of the U.S. Constitution does not have a time limit for ratification, the further the people and state legislatures go with establishing the Citizens Limit Congress Amendment by themselves:

 - the more that it will be in Congress' best interest to reduce federal government spending

 - the more that it will be in Congress' best interest to be accommodating in its relationship with the people and the state legislatures

 - the quicker that the people and state legislatures will have meaningful input in Washington after Congress crashes both our economy and our societal safety net

For 2019, Transparency International ranked the United States number twenty-three in terms of misusing public power for private benefit.

It will not be easy to eliminate a trillion dollar annual federal deficit and to start repaying the trillions of dollars in federal government debts. This is especially true if too many of the people who can create businesses and jobs for the future, decide to take their money and move to other countries, similar to what happened in Cuba a half century ago.

A financial-market revolt against our Treasury bonds can only be avoided or dealt with properly by using the Citizens Limit Congress Amendment. Without this amendment, the state legislatures and the people will be powerless while Congress, whose excessive spending will have caused the problem in the first place, drastically restructures our economy in response to the financial-market revolt.

The United States federal government currently has us $28 trillion in debt and it is getting worse by about $1 trillion a year. The $28 trillion Federal Debt excludes $10 trillion for Federal Agency Debt, $55 trillion of unfunded liabilities for Social Security and Medicare, and at least $12 trillion of unfunded liabilities for Medicaid. Eventually the federal government may be tempted to print more money to pay off the debt, which would lead to a full scale financial-market revolt against our Treasury bonds that would (1) lower the value of the U.S. dollar relative to other currencies, (2) increase the inflation rate, and (3) increase interest rates. The resulting economic crisis will make the 2008 financial crisis a warning that should not have been kicked down the road for the last 13 years. The extra debt our country took on during the last 13 years made it seem like the 2008 financial crisis was not that bad. Paying back the extra debt will have the opposite effect. The longer we continue to make short-term decisions, the longer we have to live with the consequences of short-term decisions.

If we do not get federal government spending under control soon, the eventual financial-market revolt against our Treasury bonds will be devastating. Prime U.S. businesses and properties will be bought up at relatively bargain prices by investors in countries that will then have relatively stronger currencies, especially if real high interest rates in the U.S. significantly lower demand for these assets. Many high-paying management jobs at these newly foreign-owned companies can easily be moved outside the U.S. to avoid U.S. employment laws and lawsuits.

The sale of prime U.S. businesses and properties will not reduce the federal debt or reduce the deficit spending. High interest rates in the U.S. will make the federal debt and deficit spending problems much worse. High interest rates in the U.S. will also stifle business growth, which will reduce employment and reduce tax revenues. People who carry their own weight in society will blame people who do not work hard enough. People who do not carry their own weight in society will blame people who do not pay their fair share of taxes. These two different opinions will continue to be encouraged and exploited by the two political parties that control Congress. Instead, Congress should be encouraging people to carry their own weight in society and discouraging people from not carrying their own weight in society.

If we stay on our current path and let all of this happen, the turn-of-the-millennium will likely mark the peak of U.S. civilization, caused for the most part by unsustainable economic policies.

Congress continues to bury the people further in debt, so that Washington-special-interest groups will continue to help the members of Congress stay in office and prosper.

When our state legislatures lost their constitutional right to propose amendments, they and their inhabitants lost their ability to hold on to their constitutional rights that "are reserved to the States respectively, or to the people" (quotation from Amendment X of the U.S. Constitution).

Our state legislatures have a responsibility to do what is best in the long run for those they represent.

Voters have a responsibility to consider the long-term to be more important than the short-term.

Changing the tax laws may seem to be an appealing alternative to reducing spending, but it would hardly make a dent in our debt and these tax laws are a major reason why U.S. technology entrepreneurs create so much more economic value than their European counterparts create. The other major reason is that U.S. technology companies have much more of a free hand to use value created when hiring, promoting, paying, and retaining employees than their European counterparts have.

After the Citizens Limit Congress Amendment is ratified, federal government spending programs can be limited to sustainable levels.

It would have been very good if Congress had saved the positive cash-flows from Social Security and Medicare for the inevitable negative cash-flows. It should be about what is best for the people, not what is best for the Washington-Special-Interest groups.

Our states need to use their constitutional freedoms to do things like run their own educational systems. The resulting successful educational systems and ideas in some states can then be implemented by other states.

This book was written to:

- eliminate doubts about voting results, to eliminate doubts about whether we live in a Democracy; and present a plan to implement Voting Transparency

- improve economic efficiency

- advocate for educational software where each student learns at their own pace so they can build a solid foundation and work on challenging material that they are prepared for; everyone will be able to use the software to increase their earnings

- explain the effect of increasing freedom & liberty

- compare Capitalism to Socialism

- explain importance of carrying your own weight

- raise awareness that Congress has us headed for an inevitable economic crash that will soon drastically reduce our standard of living

- prepare the people and state legislatures to have meaningful input after the crash when Congress "rebuilds" our economy and societal safety net

- prevent further erosion of our constitutional rights

- restore having the people, state legislatures, and the federal government each be subject to a check and balance from the other two

Chapter 1

Voting Transparency

U.S. Voting Transparency is the easiest and most reliable way for all and only eligible voters to vote and have their votes counted correctly.

Eliminating doubts about voting results, will eliminate doubts about whether we live in a democracy.

Federal and state voting needs to be done by citizens using their online account at socialsecurity.gov where citizens can update things like their legal name and address. SSA (Social Security Administration) and the states would jointly determine who is eligible to vote based on all federal and state information. A unique number would be assigned to each person's vote and would be on both the vote   copy that remains in the online account and the vote copy that immediately goes to the state without the voter's name.

Each voter would be able to go to their online account and see their vote as counted in the SSA voting results. There should be no differences between SSA voting results and each state's voting results.

Everyone who is eligible to vote can vote. People who cannot set up or get into their online account at socialsecurity.gov can cast a provisional vote. The provisional vote will be accepted and held confidentially by the SSA but will not be counted until the online account at socialsecurity.gov is set up and both the SSA and the state determine that the person is eligible to vote. This will delay the overall vote result for any candidate who has the most votes but would lose their race if the remaining provisional votes for the candidate are not counted and the remaining provisional votes for the candidate's opponents are all counted.

People will be able to log in to socialsecurity.gov to see if they are currently eligible to vote in the next election.

Each person's vote will remain unknown to everyone else.

There will be a record of all transactions to and from each online voting portal; this record will only be used if a person says that their vote was not counted correctly.

Hacking into someone else's voting portal will be a crime. Casting someone else's vote without their written permission and without entering, in the portal, the name of the person casting the vote, will be a crime. Looking up who voted and who did not vote will be a crime.

Anyone convicted of violating a federal or state voting law regarding this voting system, will receive a lifetime ban from having a federal job or working, directly or indirectly, under a federal contract.

Voting transparency is needed for:

- federal and state primaries
- federal and state elections
- state ballot initiatives and referendums, especially those that concern economic efficiency
- ratification of U.S. Constitutional Amendments
- use when federal government spending soon crashes our economy
- opinion surveys, so we know what the majority of voters really think
- direct democracy, for when our elected representatives are intimidated by those who use force to achieve political and social goals. Citizens need a quick and easy way to vote on changing (1) where and how government and donated money gets spent, (2) law enforcement, and (3) which laws that district attorneys can decide not to prosecute, and which laws district attorneys can prosecute more leniently for certain groups of people.

Voting Transparency is important for state ballot initiatives and referendums, especially those that concern economic efficiency.

Economic efficiency involves having businesses and government hire, promote, pay, and retain employees based on value created. This will lower costs and give everyone an incentive to develop the skills needed to maximize the value that they can create for an employer. U.S. tech companies are hiring more and more tech employees in India where employees compete, in school and on the job, for these high paying jobs.

Educational software is needed to prepare students to create value that others are willing to pay for. We need educational software, with text chatting for students' questions, that teaches all subjects for all grade levels through a two-year associate degree. Students need the option to learn from educational software where they can build a solid educational foundation and work on challenging material that they are prepared for.

Each school system could create or buy their own educational software for each subject and make it available to all U.S. students. Teachers could do the text chatting. School systems would pay each other based on which school system's software their students used for each subject.

Students could get help with their online classes from teachers or select to learn in traditional classroom settings for any or all subjects.

Each student and parent needs access and time to fully review the student's upcoming traditional classroom curriculums, before choosing between traditional classroom learning and online learning. Online learners could choose software from any other U.S. school system, for the same subjects.

Everyone would have access to the educational software, so they can increase their earnings by increasing the value that they can create for an employer.

Voting transparency can create opinion surveys that are believable.

Opinion surveys can be done for organizations that pay the SSA. The SSA will use the Voting Transparency system to survey voters as follows: An organization can request anonymous survey participants based on which votes the voter voted in and/or did not vote in, as well as which voting district the voter is registered in. The organization can decide how much, if anything, each voter gets paid, by the voting system, for their response. The organization would just get anonymous survey results by voting district. Survey responses shall never be linked to the applicable voter. This will create reliable survey results. The organization that pays for the survey can have the voting system certify any or all of (1) the selection criteria for all voters included in the survey, (2) the exact wording of everything the voters saw on their voting portal,

(3) the anonymous survey results that the organization received, and (4) the date of the survey.

Implementation of Voting Transparency involves the following:

People who support the online Voting Transparency system in this chapter, need to tell everyone else they know about this system.

People then need to contact their representatives in Congress and ask them to start working on the online Voting Transparency system in this book. The first step for Congress is to have the SSA prepare the list described below. Representatives who support it should let voters know which representatives do not support it. Eventually, Congress will set up the online Voting Transparency system for use by any or all states.

People then need to contact their state legislators and ask them to request the list below from Congress. State legislators who support it should let voters know which representatives do not support it. Eventually, the online Voting Transparency system will be used by all states.

To start working on Voting Transparency, Congress and the states need to get started on the following:

Congress needs to have the SSA maintain an up-to-date list with all Social Security numbers ever issued, with the following information for each number.

- Active or Inactive status
- U.S. Citizenship
- State of residence
- If old enough to vote in state of residence
- If disqualified from voting in state of residence for any reason other than age
- Possibly more information could be needed on the list, but nothing could go on the list that could identify a person's name or address

The list above would be based on all information that the federal government has.

The states would have access to the SSA list and would use it along with all their own state information. If the states find errors in the SSA list, the states and the SSA would work together to straighten things out. Ideally, the states will encourage their citizens to make sure their online account is set up correctly at socialsecurity.gov and that information, like address, is correct.

Congress may have to allow the states to require people to know their valid Social Security number in order to vote.

The states will need to pass laws that require people to know their valid Social Security number in order to vote.

Congress will need to have the SSA set up online voting at socialsecurity.gov

Voting using the online account at socialsecurity.gov is the easiest, safest, and least expensive way to vote. In addition, it is the best way to eliminate doubts about voting results, which will eliminate doubts about whether we live in a democracy.

Please feel free to contact this book's author with your thoughts about U.S. Voting Transparency. John@USvotingtransparency.org

Chapter 2

Article V of the U.S. Constitution

Article V of the U.S. Constitution

The Congress, whenever two thirds of both Houses shall deem it necessary, shall propose Amendments to this Constitution, or, on the Application of the Legislatures of two thirds of the several States, shall call a Convention for proposing Amendments, which, in either Case, shall be valid to all Intents and Purposes, as Part of this Constitution, when ratified by the Legislatures of three fourths of the several States, or by Conventions in three fourths thereof, as the one or the other Mode of Ratification may be proposed by the Congress; Provided that no Amendment which may be made prior to the Year One thousand eight hundred and eight shall in any Manner affect the first and fourth Clauses in the Ninth Section of the first Article; and that no State, without its Consent, shall be deprived of its equal Suffrage in the Senate.

The word "shall" as used above, is used throughout the Constitution to mean "peremptory" (absolute & unconditional).

Congress has received "the Application of the Legislatures of two thirds of the several States" many times, and just refuses to "call a Convention," as required by Article V. Quotations are from Article V above.

In The Federalist 85 quotations below, Alexander Hamilton (who wrote Article V) states that "on the application of the legislatures of two thirds of the States," Congress "will have no option" and "will be obliged" to "call a convention for proposing amendments". He also states, "The words of this article are peremptory. The congress 'shall call a convention.' Nothing in this particular is left to the discretion of that body." Interestingly, he ends the paragraph with "We may safely rely on the disposition of the State legislatures to erect barriers against the encroachments of the national authority."

Quotation below is from The Federalist 85, concerning Article V, written by Alexander Hamilton, who wrote Article V:

"In opposition to the probability of subsequent amendments, it has been urged that the persons delegated to the administration of the national government will always be disinclined to yield up any portion of the authority of which they were once possessed. For my own part I acknowledge a thorough conviction that any amendments which may, upon mature consideration, be thought useful, will be applicable to the organization of the government, not to the mass of its powers; and on this account alone, I think there is no weight in the observation just stated. I also think there is little weight in it on another account. The intrinsic difficulty of governing THIRTEEN STATES at any rate, independent of calculations upon an ordinary degree of public spirit and integrity, will, in my opinion constantly impose on the national rulers the necessity of a spirit accommodation to the reasonable expectations of their constituents. But there is yet a further consideration, which proves beyond the possibility of doubt, that the observation is futile. It is this that the national rulers, whenever nine states concur, will have no option upon the subject. By the fifth article of the plan, the Congress will be obliged "on the application of the legislatures of two thirds of the states, (which at present amounts to nine), to call a convention for proposing amendments, which shall be valid, to all intents and purposes, as part of the Constitution, when ratified by the legislatures of three fourths of the States, or by conventions in three fourths thereof " The words of this article are peremptory. The Congress "shall call a convention." Nothing in this particular is left to the discretion of that body. And of consequence, all the declamation about their disinclination to a change vanishes in air. Nor however difficult it may be supposed to unite two thirds or three fourths of the State legislatures, in amendments which may affect local interests, can there be any room to apprehend any such difficulty in a union on points which are merely relative to the general liberty or security of the people. We may safely rely on the disposition of the State legislatures to erect barriers against the encroachments of the national authority."

The four Supreme Court rulings below all concern Article V and reiterate the requirement in Article V for Congress to call a convention when the states meet the requirement in Article V to have the convention called.

•   In Dodge v. Woolsey (1855), the Supreme Court stated "people……have directed that amendments should be made representatively for them, by congress of the United States, when two thirds of both houses shall propose them; or where the legislatures of two thirds of the several states shall call a convention for proposing amendments."

•   In Hawke v. Smith (1920), the Supreme Court stated "This article makes provision for the proposal of amendments either by two-thirds of both houses of Congress or on application of the Legislatures of two-thirds of the states;…………The language of the article is plain, and admits no doubt in its interpretation. It is not the function of courts or legislative bodies, national or state, to alter the method which the Constitution has fixed."

•   In Dillon v. Gloss (1921), the Supreme Court stated, "A further mode of proposal – as yet never invoked – is provided, which is, that on the application of two thirds of the states Congress shall call a convention for the purpose."

•   In United States v. Sprague (1931), the Supreme Court stated, "The United States asserts that article 5 is clear in statement and in meaning, contains no ambiguity, and calls for no resort to rules of construction. A mere reading demonstrates that this is true. It provides two methods for proposing amendments. Congress may propose them by a vote of two-thirds of both houses, or, on the application of the legislatures of two-thirds of the states, must call a convention to propose them."

Congress ignores the above Supreme Court rulings just like they ignore their obligation to call Article V Conventions.

Chapter 3

Congress Refuses to Call an Article V Convention

Congress Unconstitutionally Refuses to Call an Article V Convention.

The states have submitted over 500 applications for an Article V Convention. Based on the requirement in Article V of the Constitution, Congress should have called an Article V Convention at least 10 times.

Congress' excuse for not calling an Article V Convention is that Congress does not have a procedure for counting the states' applications. Imagine what Alexander Hamilton's response would be to this excuse.

Article V does not contain any requirement that the state legislatures' applications for an Article V Convention be any more specific than as stated in Article V - "for proposing amendments." The convention call's only possible purpose is as stated in Article V - "for proposing amendments." If the state legislatures' applications contain additional information about specific amendments, it is nothing more than additional information. The only other convention similar enough to an Article V Convention to set a precedent for an Article V Convention is the Federal Convention of 1787 where the Constitution was written. The state legislatures' stated purposes to have this convention were "to render the constitution of the Foederal Government adequate to the exigencies of the Union" (quotation from Annapolis Convention dated September 14th, 1786) and "the necessity of extending the revision of the federal System to all its defects" (quotation from Virginia Resolution dated November 23, 1786). These two purposes are just as general as "for proposing Amendments"; therefore, there is no precedent for requiring the applications to be any more specific than "for proposing Amendments." I am not aware of Congress ever saying that the reason for not calling an Article V Convention is that the applications were not for the same subject.

Article V does not say that there is any time limit within which the applications from two-thirds of the states have to be submitted; therefore, there is no time limit. Amendment XXVII was proposed in 1789 without a time limit for ratification, and was ratified 202 years later in 1992.

Article V does not say that the state legislatures' applications can be rescinded; therefore, they cannot be rescinded. States that want to rescind their applications still have the power not to ratify any proposed amendments. When determining if three-fourths of the states had ratified Amendment XIV, Congress counted all state ratifications, including those that the state legislatures had rescinded prior to three-fourths of the states ratifying the amendment; the Supreme Court refers to this as a "historic precedent," which means that this is how it will be done in the future.

Congress unconstitutionally blocks the states from proposing amendments, as follows: Article V of the U.S. Constitution states "...on the Application of the Legislatures of two thirds of the several States, [Congress] shall call a Convention for proposing Amendments..." The word "shall" is used throughout the Constitution to mean "peremptory" (absolute & unconditional). In The Federalist 85, Alexander Hamilton (who wrote Article V) states that "on the application of the legislatures of two thirds of the States," Congress "will have no option" and "will be obliged" to "call a convention for proposing amendments." He also states, "The words of this article are peremptory. The congress "shall call a convention." "Nothing in this particular is left to the discretion of that body." During the 230 years since he wrote this, Congress has received "the Application of the Legislatures of two thirds of the several States" many times, and just refuses to "call a Convention," as required by Article V.

All states, except Hawaii, have submitted Article V applications to Congress, but Congress has never called a convention as required by the Constitution. Nothing in the Constitution says anything about the application's form, expiration date, or description of subjects to be included/excluded at the convention. Congress can make up its own rules that are not in the Constitution, concerning the application's form, expiration date, description of subjects to be included/excluded at the convention, and other matters. Congress can use these unconstitutional made-up rules to block the hundreds of state applications from 49 different states from ever adding up to 34 (two-thirds of the states).

Congress can make up these unconstitutional rules, because the Supreme Court has classified the states proposing and ratifying amendments as a "Political Question." This means that the Supreme Court will not issue a ruling against Congress concerning these unconstitutional made-up rules, which can block the states from their constitutional right to propose amendments. Our Founding Father's overriding intention concerning this matter was for the state legislatures to be able to propose amendments without being blocked by Congress.

The Supreme Court's "Political Question" doctrine would also allow Congress to both control any Article V Convention and determine whether the people's ratification of an amendment is valid. The

Supreme Court's "Political Question" doctrine appears to have three tests, all three of which must be passed, in order for a matter to fall within the "Political Question" doctrine. Proposing and ratifying amendments fails the first test because the Constitution did not give Congress any control over the states proposing amendments, or ratifying amendments, or even ratifying the U.S. Constitution. It also fails the second test, because there is a clear and usable standard for resolving the matter, which is that things clearly stated in the Constitution are constitutional. It passes the third test because the Court should avoid judicial policymaking concerning this matter. If this third test, which is the only one passed, was the only test, the courts would not interfere with Congress unconstitutionally blocking the state legislatures' constitutional right, and the courts would not interfere with the state legislatures and the people taking actions that are not unconstitutional to overcome Congress' unconstitutional actions.

The Supreme Court's selective use of its "Political Question" doctrine makes it appear that the "Political Question" doctrine was designed to disguise the Supreme Court being bullied by both Congress and the President. Perhaps, the Supreme Court should have been given more constitutional protection from political power of the legislative and executive branches of government; only a U.S. Constitutional Amendment can fix this.

Since the Supreme Court has classified the states proposing and ratifying amendments as a "Political Question," there is no judge/final authority to rule on the federal government and the state legislatures' differences concerning the state legislatures proposing amendments. Hopefully, the states will end up giving the Supreme Court enough power to not need to use its "Political Question" doctrine. Congress will not give the Supreme Court this power; Congress is the main reason why the Supreme Court had to create its "Political Question" doctrine, which has no basis in the Constitution.

Congress and the President should not have any discretion to change the number of Supreme Court Justices.

If the Supreme Court's "Political Question" doctrine causes the Supreme Court to not rule against Congress for blocking the Constitution's stated intention that the state legislatures can propose amendments, it would also cause the Supreme Court to not rule against the state legislatures concerning how the state legislatures permanently restore their constitutional right to propose amendments, without doing anything unconstitutional. This would also cause the federal courts to not issue injunctions or take other actions against the state legislatures concerning how the state legislatures and the people propose and ratify the Citizens Limit Congress Amendment. This hands-off approach would be consistent with how the federal courts have not issued injunctions or taken other actions against Congress for unconstitutionally blocking the state legislatures from their constitutional right to propose amendments. Hopefully, Congress and the state legislatures are treated evenly by the Supreme Court. Hopefully, in the unlikely event that Congress does not quickly propose the Citizens Limit Congress Amendment, the Supreme Court will make it clear right from the beginning that (1) the Supreme Court and the federal courts will not get involved in this matter and that (2) Congress does not have any constitutional authority concerning the state legislatures and the people proposing and ratifying the Citizens Limit Congress Amendment.

Chapter 4

Erosion of Constitutional Rights

The Constitution's system of checks and balances defines the power of the federal government and gives all other powers (excluding those prohibited by the Constitution) to the states and to the people. The powers given to the federal government were split up into the following three branches. Legislative power was vested in the Congress of the United States, which consists of a Senate and House of Representatives. Executive Power was vested in a President of the United States. Judicial power was vested in the Supreme Court of the United States, and in lower courts, which Congress could establish. Elected members of the Legislative and Executive branches as well as appointed members of the Supreme Court all take an oath to uphold the Constitution, including Amendments. The Constitution gave each of the groups (States/People, Congress, President, and Supreme Court) separate powers with the intention that they would all be a check and balance on each other to keep any one of them from expanding its power beyond the powers granted by the Constitution.

At first, Congress rarely tried to expand its powers because it made sure its proposed laws were constitutional. Eventually Congress started proposing laws that expanded its powers but they were vetoed by Presidents for being unconstitutional. Eventually the Presidents started going along with some unconstitutional laws but they were stopped by the Supreme Court for being unconstitutional. Eventually the Supreme Court started going along with some unconstitutional laws. At that time, the applicable check and balance had been circumvented and there was nothing in place to keep the federal government (combined Congress, President, and Supreme Court) from unconstitutionally taking power away from the states and the people.

The resulting lost powers primarily involve the Constitution's Commerce Clause, the Necessary and Proper Clause, and the Ninth and Tenth Amendments. These lost powers are well documented in scholarly books about the Constitution.

The Supreme Court's "Political Question" doctrine has made it easy for Congress to block the state legislatures from exercising their constitutional right to have their amendments proposed.

The Supreme Court's "Political Question" doctrine has enabled the federal government, primarily Congress, to expand its constitutional authority over the state legislatures and the people in matters where the Supremacy Clause was not appropriate. This doctrine is arguably necessary to protect the Supreme Court from Congress. Perhaps the Supreme Court needs more constitutional protection from Congress and from the President.

The "Political Question" doctrine has no basis in the Constitution. "Political Questions" are supposed to be resolved by the political process, not the courts. The political process involves voting for or against the applicable politicians involved in the matter and asking them to change the law. Any unconstitutional laws that result from the "Political Question" doctrine can become "precedents" that open the door for more unconstitutional laws, from Congress and from the courts. The political process will never permanently restore the state legislatures' constitutional right to propose U.S. Constitutional Amendments, in a manner that it cannot ever be blocked by the federal government again.

The Supreme Court's comments about the "Political Question" doctrine concern the "inappropriateness of court review" of "political matters" concerning legislative, executive, and state constitutional disputes. In the following three cases, the Supreme Court seems to violate its "Political Question" doctrine that existed when each matter being decided occurred.

•   In 1974, the Supreme Court ruled against President Richard M. Nixon's claim of Executive Privilege in the Watergate matter, even though it was well settled that the decisions of the President and other executive officials are protected from the federal courts (United States v. Nixon).

•   In 1944, the Supreme Court ruled that the House of Representatives had to include a duly elected member who was constitutionally qualified; even though Article I of the Constitution says that, each house shall be the judge of the qualifications of its members (Powell v. McCormack).

•   In 1962, the Supreme Court ruled to allow a challenge to how the Tennessee legislature apportioned its voting districts (Baker v. Carr).

Chapter 5

Checks and Balances

When the federal government was being planned, our Founding Fathers knew that there was the possibility that the federal government would try to expand its powers.

Fortunately, our Founding Fathers listed everything in the Constitution that the federal government was authorized to do and said everything else, excluding things forbidden by the Constitution, was left for the states and the people.

Unfortunately, Congress does not always interpret the Constitution's words and phrases according to their meaning at the time of enactment. Also, Congress seems to have coerced the Supreme Court into creating its "Political Question" doctrine, which enables Congress to do more things that our founding fathers would presumably consider unconstitutional.

Fortunately, our Founding Fathers put a check and balance in Article V of the Constitution for situations like this. Two-thirds of the state legislatures can go to Congress and have Congress call a convention where the state legislatures can propose a U.S. Constitutional Amendment, which can be ratified by a majority vote in each of at least three-fourths of the states.

Unfortunately, Congress just refuses to call a convention for the state legislatures to propose amendments, even though two-thirds of the state legislatures have properly applied many times for the convention as specified in Article V of the Constitution. Every state except Hawaii has requested an Article V Convention, and in total, over 500 such requests have been made to Congress. Nothing in Article V says that the requests have to be within a set time-period or that they need to be for the same subject.

Article V of the Constitution says "Congress Shall call a convention for proposing Amendments". The word Shall is used throughout the Constitution for things that are "peremptory" (which means absolute & unconditional).

In The Federalist 85, Alexander Hamilton (who wrote Article V) states that "on the application of the legislatures of two thirds of the States," Congress "will have no option" and "will be obliged" to "call a convention for proposing amendments." He also states, "The words of this article are peremptory. The congress "shall call a convention." "Nothing in this particular is left to the discretion of that body."

In The Federalist 85, Alexander Hamilton goes on to say, "We may safely rely on the disposition of the State legislatures to erect barriers against the encroachments of the national authority."

In summary, Alexander Hamilton seems to be saying (1) that Congress cannot block the state legislatures from proposing amendments and (2) the amendment process is how the states will erect barriers against encroachments of the national authority.

All that is needed to permanently restore the state legislatures' constitutional right to propose amendments is to add an amendment to our Constitution that permanently restores the state legislatures' constitutional right to propose amendments, in a manner that it cannot ever be blocked by the federal government again. The question is how to add such an amendment when Congress refuses to fulfill its constitutional duty to call a convention where the state legislatures can propose the amendment.

Fortunately, our Founding Fathers left another check and balance that Congress cannot re-interpret as they do with the Constitution's words and phrases, and Congress cannot unconstitutionally block as they do to the convention where state legislatures should be able to propose amendments.

When the people established their U.S. Federal Government, they also established the Article V and Article VII checks and balances. This enabled the people, working with their state legislatures, to always keep enough control to prevent Congress from doing anything significantly detrimental to our country, like crashing both our economy and societal safety net.

There is nothing that is even close to being as dangerous to our Constitution as Congress crashing both our economy and societal safety net and then Congress "rebuilding" both our economy and societal safety net without any meaningful input from the state legislatures and the people. Congress will remain unable to stand up to the Washington-special-interest groups and will continue down the same path, increasing federal debt, increasing unfunded federal mandates, and building more inefficiencies into our economy. In addition, Congress will use the "national emergency," caused by the crash, to encroach further on our U.S. Constitutional Rights. Our standard of living will fall significantly relative to the rest of the world. Our societal safety net will probably never grow to the inflation-adjusted sustainable level it could have been maintained at.

The Citizens Limit Congress Amendment will:

- enable people and state legislatures to reduce federal government spending

- enable people and state legislatures to redirect federal government spending, with a majority vote of people in each of any three-fourths of the states or by state legislatures in each of any three-fourths of the states, respectively

- enable people to propose U.S. Constitutional Amendments by a majority vote of people in each of any two-thirds of the states that can be fully ratified by state legislatures in each of any three-fourths of the states

- enable state legislatures in each of any two-thirds of the states to propose U.S. Constitutional Amendments that can be fully ratified by a majority vote of people in each of any three-fourths of the states

- restore the Constitution's check and balance on the federal government with changes to the check and balance so that it can never again be blocked by the federal government

 - be the only way we have to limit Congress from crashing then "rebuilding" our economy/societal safety net and then using the "national emergency" caused by the crash, to further reduce our constitutional rights

Enabling people to propose amendments is required to make sure that the people's ideas for amendments are considered.

Enabling people and state legislatures to propose amendments and ratify each other's proposed amendments is critical to protect the people and state legislatures' constitutional rights forever.

All of the above can be established by people and state legislatures, the same way they established the U.S. Constitution. Congress will make this unnecessary by proposing the Citizens Limit Congress Amendment that people and state legislatures get close to establishing without federal government involvement. By doing this, Congress will keep the Article VII Check and Balance unused and make it much less likely to ever be needed.

Article. VII. of the Constitution states - "The Ratification of the Conventions of nine States, shall be sufficient for the Establishment of this Constitution between the States so ratifying the Same."

The Constitution, with the addition of the states' Citizens Limit Congress Amendment and the other 27 amendments, just needs to be ratified by state conventions; the more state ratifications, the more accommodating that Congress will be.

Before ratification by two-thirds of the states, Congress will propose the states' Citizens Limit Congress Amendment for three-fourths of the states to ratify as an amendment. The Article VII Check and Balance will remain unused and it will become much less likely to be ever needed.

If the people in each of any two-thirds or more of the states did ratify the Constitution as above, it would not break the rules and agreements that maintain the perpetual union of the states. Instead, it would restore the state legislatures' constitutional right to propose amendments, in a manner that this constitutional right can never again be blocked by the federal government. Future historians would blame Congress for forcing the state legislatures and the people to use the Article VII Check and Balance to restore this constitutional right.

If the Article VII Check and Balance did get used as above, it would uphold the Constitution by (1) ratifying the Constitution and all existing amendments and (2) reusing Article VII to restore the state legislatures' constitutional right to propose amendments, in a manner that this constitutional right cannot ever be blocked by the federal government again. Congress is not upholding the Constitution when Congress refuses to call Article V Conventions that two-thirds of the state legislatures have properly applied for many times.

Congress cannot use the supremacy clause or anything else to block ratification by the people in each of any two-thirds of the states, just like the Continental Congress could not have used the first sentence in Article XIII of the Articles of Confederation or anything else to block the Constitution if only two-thirds of the states had ratified it.

When Article VII of the Constitution was written, the decision was made by an 8 to 3 vote to not require Congress' approval of the Constitution.

It should also be noted that (1) Congress was never asked to approve the Constitution, (2) Congress never approved the Constitution, and (3) Congress never said that they approved the Constitution.

The restriction in the Constitution on the states entering into a Treaty, Alliance, or Confederation with other states was also in the Articles of Confederation.

The first sentence of Article VI of the Constitution never applied to the states.

The Supreme Court's "political question" doctrine, which has no basis in the Constitution, prevents the Supreme Court from ruling that Congress shall call an Article V Convention that two-thirds of the state legislatures have properly applied for. Fortunately, consistent application of the Supreme Court's "political question" doctrine would prevent the federal government from interfering with the state legislature and the people's use of Article VII to restore the state legislatures' constitutional right to propose amendments, in a manner that this constitutional right can never again be blocked by the federal government. It (1) uses the political process of voting by the people, (2) is done the same way as the Constitution was ratified, (3) is a matter that the state legislatures and the people, just like for the Constitution, are the only segments of government involved, and (4) does not involve any judicial policymaking by the Supreme Court.

Our liberties need to be protected from people who profit by taking away our liberties. The Citizens Limit Congress Amendment protects our liberties by (1) restoring the constitutional check and balance on the federal government and (2) giving us a system that increases our control over how our money is spent.

We are way past the tipping point between the following:

 - the risk and consequence of what will happen when the financial-market revolt against our Treasury bonds ends up crashing both our economy and societal safety net

 - the risk and consequence of what will happen when the constitutional check and balance on the federal government is permanently restored and the people have a system that increases their control over how their money is spent

Article VII of our Constitution was written to allow as few as two-thirds of the states to ratify a new Constitution that would then go into effect for them, as well as go into effect for any other states that ratified it. This check and balance protects the Article V check and balance, which is being unconstitutionally blocked by the federal government. When the federal government, which was created by the Constitution, went into operation, two of the states had not ratified the Constitution. Establishment of the Constitution made the Articles of Confederation null and void for the states that ratified the Constitution. These states did not fulfill and did not need to fulfill the requirements in the Articles of Confederation for replacing, amending, and/or altering the Articles of Confederation.

When Congress proposes the Citizens Limit Congress Amendment, they will designate ratification by the state legislatures, in order to move things along as quickly as possible. Congress will not want to be responsible for any delays that could be blamed for keeping the people from preventing the crash of both the economy and societal safety net. Normally, money from Washington-special-interest groups gets split-up and used for misleading political advertisements that basically offset each other. If these groups worked together against ratification by the people, these groups' misleading political advertisements could sabotage the will of the people and would alienate Congress from the people and from the state legislatures.

After two-thirds of the states ratify the Constitution, with the addition of the states' Citizens Limit Congress Amendment and the other 27 amendments, the remaining states would ratify it quickly, for the following two reasons. First, states that are the first to ratify it will be recorded in history as the leaders while any holdout states, if any, will not be looked upon as favorably. Second, if I lived in a holdout state, if there are any, I would feel like a second-class person versus people whose states restored their constitutional rights; consequently, I would vote against my state legislators who opposed ratification.

Chapter 6

Preserving Society's Safety Net

Either:

Scenario 1 - Federal government spending programs are reduced to sustainable levels so our societal safety net can be maintained at a sustainable level for the long-term.

or

Scenario 2 - Federal government spending programs cause a financial market revolt against our Treasury bonds, which will cause a crash of both our economy and our societal safety net. It would then take decades before our societal safety net grows to the sustainable level it could have been maintained at, if the state legislatures had permanently restored their constitutional right to propose amendments and then curtailed unfunded federal mandates and limited federal government spending programs to sustainable levels.

Prospects for Scenario 1 above are currently dim, because the same forces that are causing the increasing federal debt are also resisting reductions in spending.

The only hope for implementing Scenario 1 above is as follows:

- The federal government caused the federal deficit and federal debt, and the federal government will not reduce spending on its own. The state legislatures and the people need to be able to reduce federal government spending, such as "no more unfunded federal mandates."

- The state legislatures and the people need to be prepared, in case the federal government crashes the economy and the federal government wants to rebuild the economy without the state legislatures and the people's meaningful input.

- We need a sustainable societal safety net for, among other things, everyone who did not get on the right track that leads to being a productive adult. The societal safety net needs to be expanded to provide in-home counseling for these people and others when they start having babies, so their children will get on the right track and be ready for pre-school/head-start programs.

- We need to expand daycare subsidies for people on public aid, young girls, and low-income people so they can join the workforce and set good examples for future generations.

- The state legislatures need to permanently restore their constitutional right to propose amendments, which Congress is unconstitutionally blocking.

- The Article VII Check and Balance enables the state legislatures to permanently restore their constitutional right to propose amendments, by using the Citizens Limit Congress Amendment.

- The state legislatures need to start asking Congress to propose the Citizens Limit Congress Amendment, so Congress can make it unnecessary for the state legislatures to use the Article VII Check and Balance.

- The Citizens Limit Congress Amendment has nothing to do with the two main political parties, both of which prefer an overly centralized federal government, which historically leads to countries' declines.

- It takes two-thirds of the state legislatures to even propose an amendment, which is a better safeguard for the people than the 50% majority that Congress can use to pass laws.

If the state legislatures do not work hard enough to establish the Citizens Limit Congress Amendment, they will end up being forever criticized by historians for letting things fall apart. The window of opportunity will not remain open much longer.

The Citizens Limit Congress Amendment has to be ratified before the state legislatures and the people have any meaningful input in how the federal government reduces spending and "rebuilds" the economy.

Chapter 7

Capitalism with Competition and Free Markets vs Socialism

Capitalism with competition and free markets is like Democracy. Neither are perfect, and each is much better than all its alternatives.

Capitalism with competition and free markets provides goods and services that people want at prices that maximize the value of what people can purchase. This maximization of value results from (1) incentivizing investors to make investments that create value for customers, (2) incentivizing business owners to increase value they create for their customers, and (3) incentivizing employees to get the education, work skills, and people skills needed to maximize the value they create for employers. These three incentives create the most efficient production of goods and services that customers want at prices that maximize the value of what people can purchase.

Socialist governments do not have the three incentives above and they are slow to change their production (1) for changes in available raw materials and (2) to meet their customers' changing needs and wants. These five inefficiencies and others are why socialist governments quickly run out of other people's money to spend. Then each socialist government becomes like a giant corporation, without any competition, that controls everything from how much they pay themselves and their supporters to how much everyone else gets paid and taxed. Recovery from this is difficult. People who complain about the government can easily lose their job. The percentage of voters who do not carry their own weight in society will have grown and they will be told that reductions in inflation-adjusted welfare are being caused by rich people who do not pay their fair share of taxes. Class warfare will distract people from focusing on the real problem, which is socialism. The more that a country transfers money from people who work to people who choose not to work, the less of an incentive there is to work, and the more socialistic the country becomes. The increasing percentage of voters who have fallen for the socialist slogans is alarming. Increasing taxes will reduce the three incentives in the first paragraph, which will (1) make things more expensive to buy and (2) reduce taxable income as production slows down. The reduced taxable income can only be offset by raising tax rates. The more socialistic the U.S. becomes, the harder it will be to borrow the money needed to finance the federal government debt, which is currently over $28 trillion and growing by over $1 trillion a year. The $28 trillion Federal Debt excludes $10 trillion for Federal Agency Debt, $55 trillion of unfunded liabilities for Social Security and Medicare, and at least $12 trillion of unfunded liabilities for Medicaid. We keep going farther and farther out on the slippery slope of socialism, because our schools do not teach the history of socialism. Remember what is happening in Venezuela, a country with the largest known oil reserves in the world. Remember what happened in Cuba (under Castro), China (under Mao Zedong), Germany (under Adolf Hitler and the National Socialist German Worker's Party), and Russia (under Lenin and then Stalin).

Capitalism and socialism are not sexist or racist. Capitalists try to hire people whose cost will be less than the value that the people create for their employer. Socialists seem to hire people primarily based on ideology and political affiliation.

Capitalists' innovations make life better in capitalist societies as well as in socialist societies. Without the benefit of innovations from capitalist societies, socialism would stagnate in comparison to capitalism.

The more centralized governments become, the less efficient they will usually become, because innovators will be replaced with government bureaucrats. Governments typically get more centralized, as the government people in power tend to want more power so they can make more money.

Suppose you live on a river and live off the fish that you catch. Further suppose that someone moves in next to you and asks you to share part of your catch with them every day. The short-term nice thing to do would be to share your catch with the person every day. The long-term nice thing to do would be to teach the person how to fish, which the person will eventually realize was in the person's best interest. Your neighbor has the right to an equal opportunity to earn a living. Your neighbor does not have the right to an equal result, whereby each of you would get one-half of the total fish that the two of you catch each day. Taxes collected by a government that provides the same services to each of you, should be paid by each of you equally (such as two fish a day), regardless of how productive each of you are. The less that a person gets to live off the earnings of others, the harder the person will generally work. The more that a person gets to keep their earnings, the harder the person will generally work. The harder we all work, the stronger our economy.

Chapter 8

Democracy and Liberty

The net benefits of democracy, for its people and for the world, make it undoubtedly the best form of government. A look at the lifecycles of former democracies can provide insights into how the United States got to where it is today and where it is headed without the Citizens Limit Congress Amendment. At first, the new government was restricted so it could not become like the English government that it replaced. This led to prosperity. At this point in time, mistrust of the government seemed generally inappropriate, which made it easy for government to ignore the restrictions placed on it. By continually increasing excessive social spending and crony capitalism, our federal elected politicians had a safe and easy way to increase their chance of staying in office and prospering. There is nothing to limit this spending when it is more than offset by its net long-term cost. This spending cannot be limited by how much of the taxpayers' money is in the national treasury, because the government can just keep borrowing more and more money to be repaid by future generations. Excessive social spending creates a disincentive to stay in school and to work hard on a job. Crony capitalism builds inefficiencies into our economy, in return for campaign assistance and other favors to our federal elected politicians from those who benefit from the crony capitalism. The greater the social spending and the greater the crony capitalism, the more dependency each causes, which accelerates their growth. Those advocating for excessive social spending and for crony capitalism can get the help they want, in exchange for campaign contributions and other assistance. Excessive social spending must be limited based on its net long-term costs and crony capitalism must be ended, both of which can only be done with the Citizens Limit Congress Amendment.

Increasing economic freedom and liberty is the best way to increase economic output. Also, when people have freedom and liberty, they are in a position to realize that the benefits they receive from society are much greater than society's cost is to them. This can lead to the realization that the more they are respected for carrying their own weight and for being a good person, the better they will feel about themselves.

Government force is needed to protect individuals' freedoms and liberties. Unfortunately, government force is also being used to reduce individuals' freedoms and liberties, such as in the following: Congress is burying us in debt to enrich Washington-special-interest groups that enable our elected representatives to stay in office and prosper. The Citizens Limit Congress Amendment is needed to permanently restore the Constitution's check and balance on the federal government with changes to the check and balance so that it can never again be blocked by the federal government

If the financial-markets revolt against our U.S. Treasury bonds, it will be devastating for the worldwide economy. The democratic United Nations will then likely try to expand upon its global governance ideas as the solution for the future. The majority of United Nations member countries receive more from the United Nations than they pay, and will likely be in favor of this United Nations global governance solution for the future. The United Nations was established with three main purposes, which are "to maintain international peace and security," develop "equal rights and self-determination of people," and promote "respect for human rights and for fundamental freedoms for all without distinction as to race, sex, language, or religion." In less than 75 years, the United Nations now seems to act as if its main purpose is to redistribute income without any apparent regard for the net long-term effect. It should be noted that the U.S. President, with just

the Senate's approval, can sign a treaty that allows
the United Nations to directly tax U.S. people.

Chapter 9

Economic Efficiency

We will all have to work together to get through whatever financial correction is ahead and also to get our society back on the right track. The different cultures in the United States need to have a common core whereby everyone is: (1) an individual who is not discriminated against by others or by the government, (2) an individual who has an equal opportunity to succeed or fail, (3) an individual who is only judged based upon the individual's character, which is only based upon what the individual has done, (4) an individual who is responsible for their own actions, (5) an individual who has the right to live and let live, (6) an individual who gets rewarded economically based on their net economic contribution to the nation's economy. Our core culture needs to empower individuals to be responsible adults, who carry their own weight in society.

People who are not interested in good advice concerning how to get their work done, are often more interested in having their work done by others. It would be interesting to measure the percentage of people in the U.S. who carry their own weight versus the percentage of people in China who carry their own weight.

The less that a person gets to live off the earnings of others, the harder the person will generally work. The more that a person gets to keep their earnings, the harder the person will generally work. The harder we all work, the stronger our economy will be.

Everything has to be done to get everyone working hard at creating value that others are willing to pay for. No one has a right to be paid more than the value they create for their employer, which is measured based on the cost of alternative ways the employer has to create the value.

To strengthen our economy, we need an educational system that gives each student an equal opportunity to acquire knowledge and develop the work skills needed to maximize the value that they can create for an employer. The key factor for this is that everyone must have an equal opportunity to succeed or fail. We must abolish all discrimination based on religion, race, sex, national origin, political affiliation, health, and on any other such basis, so everyone will be equally incentivized to do their best in school and on the job.

The best way to incentive students to maximize the value that they can create for an employer is as follows: Employers, like professional sports teams, should be able to hire, pay, promote, and retain employees based on the employer's assessment of the value each employee creates for the employer. Students need this opportunity, so that the harder they work in school and on the job, the more that they will earn. As a society, we need all students to have this opportunity, because the smarter and more hard working our workforce is, the stronger our economy will be.

Affirmative Action is needed in schools to offset the belief that it is not worthwhile to work hard, which was caused by unfair laws, regulations, and practices. This belief was specifically caused by things like (1) Jim Crow laws, (2) U.S. Supreme Court's Civil Rights cases in 1883 concerning Amendments 13 and 14, (3) Destruction of successful African-American businesses and communities, such as in New York 1863, Atlanta 1906, East St Louis 1917, Chicago 1919, Washington DC 1919, Knoxville 1919, Tulsa 1921, Rosewood 1923, (4) Treatment of African-American soldiers after World War 1 & 2, and (5) an inadequate educational system.

Economic efficiency involves having businesses and government hire, promote, pay, and retain employees based on value created. This will lower costs and give everyone an incentive to develop the skills needed to maximize the value that they can create for an employer. U.S. tech companies are hiring more and more tech employees in India where employees compete, in school and on the job, for these high paying jobs.

Educational software is needed to prepare students to create value that others are willing to pay for. We need educational software, with text chatting for students' questions, that teaches all subjects for all grade levels through a two-year associate degree. Students need the option to learn from educational software where they can build a solid educational foundation and work on challenging material that they are prepared for.

Each school system could create or buy their own educational software for each subject and make it available to all U.S. students. Teachers could do the text chatting. School systems would pay each other based on which school system's software their students used for each subject.

Students could get help with their online classes from teachers or select to learn in traditional classroom settings for any or all subjects.

Each student and parent needs access and time to fully review the student's upcoming traditional classroom curriculums, before choosing between traditional classroom learning and online learning. Online learners could choose software from any other U.S. school system, for the same subjects.

Everyone would have access to the educational software, so they can increase their earnings by increasing the value that they can create for an employer.

Notes concerning the educational software above:

-All words used in the lessons can be highlighted and then reviewed in a drop-down box with definition, thesaurus information, and examples of how the words are used in sentences.

-Students will be able to remotely work on group projects using their PCs.

-Students will only be able to move to the next lesson in a subject by passing a test on their PC that can only be taken at school, without any assistance.

-Each subject will have completion dates for each lesson so that students can stay on track to complete all lessons for each subject by the end of the school year.

-There will be no limit on how far ahead a student can go in the subjects. A fifth grader could be doing high school work and a high school student could earn a two-year Associate Degree.

High School students who do not score high enough on college entrance exams to be admitted, should be able to repeat whatever high school classes they need at no cost. College graduates who do not score high enough on employer exams to be hired, should be able to repeat whatever college/university classes they need at no cost. Affirmative Action in education will still be needed when high school graduates and college graduates can repeat needed classes at no cost.

In order to reduce discrimination against equally qualified potential employees, companies should be offered the following safe-harbor. The safe-harbor would allow them to hire people, without any legal risk, based on employment test results concerning skills the employer needs the people to have. In order to qualify for the safe-harbor, the companies would need to create computer-based tutorials that teach all the skills covered in the tests. The tutorials would need to be available to everyone, without any cost. Junior colleges should have classes that students can repeat as many times as they want, at no cost, that teach what is in these tutorials. The employment test would be administered by the employer. Anonymous test results, along with the average test score for the version of the test, would be available with the potential employer's name and the test taker's degrees received from which schools. This will enable prospective students to rank schools for the types of companies they want to work for. It will also be an incentive for schools to teach students the work skills needed by employers.

In order to judge people based on their character, instead of race, religion, gender, etc, there needs to be a better way than the following: Animals, including all people, who encounter others, make quick automatic assessments based on similar encounters that they have had or heard about. These automatic assessments of other people, reinforce stereotypes that are not based on the character of the person being assessed. People who stereotype other people, often get stereotyped in return, which further reinforces stereotypes that are not based on people's character. No one should judge another person based on the person's race, religion, gender, etc. Everyone should be judged based only on their character, which can only be based on what the person has done. When meeting a stranger, everyone should follow the Golden Rule - "Treat Other People, the way You want Other People to treat You".

Charter schools, such as those serving New York students from the middle of Harlem, South Bronx, and Bedford Stuyvesant are achieving extraordinary results. They are proof that the desire and ability to climb the ladder of economic success is widespread in every cross-section of children in our country.

Business Writing

Writing is an art. Often people who cannot write well are unaware of how this deficiency is limiting their career growth. The ten steps in this chapter cover how to write a business email.

1. Establish the goals of the communication, which usually involve one or more of the following:

   • Get permission

   • Confirm something

   • Explain something

   • Answer someone

   • Inform someone

   • Ask for a decision

   • Get someone to do something

2. Make sure an email is the best method to accomplish the goals. Possibly, a phone call or visit to the person would be better than an email. Talking to a person is usually better when you need questions answered before you can finish the communication. In addition, talking can be a quicker way to communicate something. You can always later use an email to confirm matters agreed upon verbally.

3. Determine the subject that goes at the top of the email. It should be a concise overview of the

email's main subject matter. It is a good place to get information conveyed such as "Revised Budget Timetable with Earlier Due Dates." Information in the subject should also be included in the text of the email, usually at the beginning.

4. Determine who should be copied on the email. Plan to send a copy of your email to everyone who needs or would want to be informed. Put yourself in the shoes of the following people and determine if you would want to be copied on the email:

   • Your boss

   • The recipient's boss

   • Others involved with the subject matter of the email

   • Others whom you make comments about in the email, such as what they said or did

Before copying anyone, make sure there is no confidential information in your email or in any emails you are replying to or forwarding.

5. Explain the current situation:

   • You should give the recipient any background information needed to understand the current situation. Give the information either right after or before you state your goals.

- Where applicable, your explanation may need to discretely clear up any doubts concerning whether you made any mistakes.

6. Explain the changes you want made to the current situation. Explain the changes as they relate to the current situation. Where applicable, your explanation needs to explain why the changes should be made.

7. Write a concise, easy-to-understand email:

- Try to start the email with your goal such as the following:
   - I would like to get your permission/agreement/approval to proceed …
   - I would like to confirm…
   - I would like to explain…
   - In response to your question about…
   - I thought you would like to know…
   - I need/would like/would appreciate your decision concerning…
   - I need/would like/would appreciate your help on…

- Avoid needlessly repeating information the recipient already knows about the subject. Make sure you include all relevant information the recipient may not know or may not have readily available. Also, include other information you want the recipient to know about.

- Write the email as if you were writing a script you would read to the person, where the person cannot respond or ask a question. Make sure the person would easily understand what you read.

- Look at the subject of the email from the recipient's point of view.

- Rough out an outline that includes all the material you need to cover. Break up the material into main thoughts that convey your message (accomplishes your goal). Each main thought should ideally become a paragraph in the email. The first sentence of each paragraph should contain the main thought and be supported by the rest of the paragraph; this helps make the email easy to scan. Add an introduction and a summary, where applicable. Recipient needs to be able to scan the email and know what to do, as follows: read it, toss it, file it, forward it, reply to it, or put it away for later.

- Organize the sections of your email. Sections that are more important should usually go first. Similar and related sections should usually go together. Keep in mind that *accomplishing your goal* is the most important factor concerning how the sections are organized.

- Write to the point. The more words you use to say something, the harder the recipient has to work to get your point.

- Make sure you answer any questions, objections, or criticisms that may occur to the recipient while reading your email.

- Avoid sarcasm.

- Use short sentences along with words the recipient will understand.

- Suppose you write about an "ABC Report." Later in the same paragraph, refer to it as the "report" or the "ABC Report" not the "study" or "analysis" or "presentation."

- Whenever you use words that have more than one meaning, like "incorporate," only use one of the meanings for the word throughout your email.

- Underline key points or use bold print, as appropriate.

- Try to avoid having two consecutive sentences or paragraphs that start with the same word.

- Be sensitive to people's feelings. Replace words like *manpower* with *staffing requirement* and avoid all generalizations, even if you think they are favorable.

- Be grammatically correct as listed below. Generally, only the first six or seven items below apply to most business emails. Use the spelling and grammar tool available in your email program.

  o Use plural and singular verbs to go with plural and singular nouns, respectively, as follows: "Jack and Tom are..." and "Jack or Tom is..."

  o Generally, use the word *good* when referring to a *noun* and use the word *well* when referring to a *verb*. Note that the second letter of *good* and *noun* are the same, and that the second letter of *well* and *verb* are the same.

  o Never start a sentence with "And" at the beginning.

  o Never start a sentence with "Because" when you are finishing a thought in the preceding sentence. The following sentence is acceptable: "Because it rained, we canceled the picnic." I would recommend replacing "Because" with "Since" in the sentence.

  o Sentences that begin with "When" or "If" should have the resulting consequence after a comma.

  o Sentences should read correctly when all words enclosed in parentheses are ignored.

o   Do not end a sentence with a preposition, such as above, across, after, between, beyond, down, for, in, near, out, past, to, up, and with.

o   For sentences that have an "or" or "and," make sure they read correctly when the "or" or "and" is deleted along with either of the two things separated by the "or" or "and." For example, the need for the italicized words in the two following sentences is clear, when the underlined words are deleted:

   ▪ I have never *done* or even considered doing it.

   ▪ I know someone *who has* and have read about people who have this ability.

o   Use plural and singular pronouns to go with plural and singular antecedent nouns, respectively, as follows: "An intern must work hard if he/she (not they) want to get hired for a full-time position."

o   A sentence should only be first person (I), second person (you), or third person (he, she, and they). Never change between first, second, or third person within a sentence.

o   Try to write using active verbs rather than passive verbs. With active verbs, the subject does the verb action. With passive verbs, the subject receives the verb action. For example, "the car hit the tree" is better than "the tree was hit by the car."

Note: A style manual, which is available at most bookstores, will have an answer for just about every question concerning grammar, punctuation, and writing in general.

8. Treat recipients appropriately:

- Make sure the tone of the email is correct. Do not *tell* a customer or a boss to do anything. In general, consideration and politeness are almost always appreciated by everyone.

- Never send an email telling someone at your level in the company to do something, especially if you are copying others on the email. It will appear that you are trying to put yourself into a position of authority over someone at your level. It is best to discuss with the person at your level what needs to be done and confirm it in an email, if necessary.

9. Make sure the email accomplishes your goals. Read the email as if you were the recipient and see if any changes are needed to accomplish your goals.

10. Proofread before sending:

- After writing the email, see if you need to revise whom you are copying.

- Before sending, read the email as though you were the recipient and each person you are sending a copy to, such as your boss. Make sure there is nothing you may later regret not revising. Be sure you are clearly conveying everything you want to convey.

- Slowly read the email word by word to catch errors. Others will form opinions of your work based on your emails, especially when you first start working at a company.

- When proofreading anything you write, keep in mind that you are building a picture in the reader's mind. The key to building a clear picture is to apply the following rules:

  o Where applicable, start with an overview of the information you are conveying.

  o State things in the order they occurred, are occurring, or will occur. For example, do not write, "The power went out when I was almost done with the project." When the readers read that the power went out, they should already know that you were almost done with the project.

  o The readers should not be misled. For example, after reading four words into the following sentence, the readers think Joe felt the sign. "Joe felt the sign was appropriate." This misleading sentence can be cleared up by inserting the word *that* after the word *felt*.

o Do not leave gaps in the picture readers are building in their mind by raising questions that go unanswered. For example, do not state, "His opinion was the same as Mary's opinion," unless you are providing, or ideally have already provided, sufficient information on Mary or her opinion. Another example is the use of technical terms the readers may not understand.

o If you are leading a reader from one thought to another, such as "since this is true the following is true," make sure the connection is clear to the reader; provide an explanation, if necessary.

Remember that once you send an email, it may be irretrievable. Others, including people outside your company, can end up seeing anything you send.

Chapter 10

Check and Balance on Congress

The Article VII Check and Balance is the "two-thirds of the states" Check and Balance that protects the Article V "three-fourths of the states" Check and Balance.

The Article VII Check and Balance is the only way the states have to permanently restore their constitutional right to propose U.S. Constitutional Amendments, in a manner that it cannot ever be blocked by the federal government again. The Article VII Check and Balance would enable the state legislatures and the people to overcome any of the following:

- Two-thirds of the state legislatures have properly applied many times for an Article V Convention, and Congress refuses to call the convention. See the "Congress Refuses to Call an Article V Convention" chapter for details.

- Congress could claim that its past refusal to call an Article V Convention is now a historical precedent, which Congress can follow in the future. The Supreme Court would not get involved.

- If an Article V Convention is called, Congress could interfere and manipulate its proceedings. The Supreme Court would not get involved.

 - The federal government could rule that Article V Convention delegates are federal officeholders, subject to federal rules and controls.

- If a majority of voters in each of at least three-fourths of the states ratify an amendment proposed by the state legislatures, Congress could disqualify the ratification. In Coleman v. Miller, the Supreme Court held that Congress had the final authority to determine the validity of an amendment's ratification.

- If a majority of voters in each of at least three-fourths of the states ratify an amendment proposed by the state legislatures, Congress could refuse to promulgate the amendment. In Coleman v. Miller, the Supreme Court held that Congress was in charge of promulgation a ratified amendment.

The Article VII check and balance enables the people, working with their state legislatures, to always keep enough control to prevent Congress from doing anything significantly detrimental to our country, like crashing both our economy and societal safety net.

The Citizens Limit Congress Amendment will:

- enable people and state legislatures to reduce federal government spending

- enable people and state legislatures to redirect federal government spending, with a majority vote of people in each of any three-fourths of the states or by state legislatures in each of any three-fourths of the states, respectively

- enable people to propose U.S. Constitutional Amendments by a majority vote of people in each of any two-thirds of the states that can be fully ratified by state legislatures in each of any three-fourths of the states

- enable state legislatures in each of any two-thirds of the states to propose U.S. Constitutional Amendments that can be fully ratified by a majority vote of people in each of any three-fourths of the states

- restore the Constitution's check and balance on the federal government with changes to the check and balance so that it can never again be blocked by the federal government

 - be the only way we have to limit Congress from crashing then "rebuilding" our economy/societal safety net and then using the "national emergency" caused by the crash, to further reduce our constitutional rights

Enabling people to propose amendments is required to make sure that the people's ideas for amendments are considered.

Enabling people and state legislatures to propose amendments and ratify each other's proposed amendments is critical to protect the people and state legislatures' constitutional rights forever.

All of the above can be established by people and state legislatures, the same way they established the U.S. Constitution. Congress will make this unnecessary by proposing the Citizens Limit Congress Amendment that people and state legislatures get close to establishing without federal government involvement. By doing this, Congress will keep the Article VII Check and Balance unused and make it much less likely to ever be needed.

Article. VII. of the Constitution states - "The Ratification of the Conventions of nine States, shall be sufficient for the Establishment of this Constitution between the States so ratifying the Same."

The Constitution, with the addition of the states' Citizens Limit Congress Amendment and the other 27 amendments, just needs to be ratified by state conventions; the more state ratifications, the more accommodating that Congress will be.

Before ratification by two-thirds of the states, Congress will propose the states' Citizens Limit Congress Amendment for three-fourths of the states to ratify as an amendment. The Article VII Check and Balance will remain unused and it will become much less likely to be ever needed.

If the people in each of any two-thirds or more of the states did ratify the Constitution as above, it would <u>not</u> break the rules and agreements that maintain the perpetual union of the states. Instead, it would restore the state legislatures' constitutional right to propose amendments, in a manner that this constitutional right can never again be blocked by the federal government. Future historians would blame Congress for forcing the state legislatures and the people to use the Article VII Check and Balance to restore this constitutional right.

If the Article VII Check and Balance did get used as above, it would uphold the Constitution by (1) ratifying the Constitution and all existing amendments and (2) reusing Article VII to restore the state legislatures' constitutional right to propose amendments, in a manner that this constitutional right cannot ever be blocked by the federal government again. Congress is not upholding the Constitution when Congress refuses to call Article V Conventions that two-thirds of the state legislatures have properly applied for many times.

Congress cannot use the supremacy clause or anything else to block ratification by the people in each of any two-thirds of the states, just like the Continental Congress could not have used the first sentence in Article XIII of the Articles of Confederation or anything else to block the Constitution if only two-thirds of the states had ratified it.

When the wording that became part of Article VII was written, the decision was made for the Constitution to not require Congress' approval of the Constitution. Based on James Madison's Notes of the Constitutional Convention (August 30 & 31, 1787): "Mr. Dickinson asked whether the concurrence of Congress is to be essential to the establishment of the system [Constitution]." There is no record in the notes of any discussion concerning this question. The next day it was suggested that the wording include, "This Constitution shall be laid before the U— S. in Congs. assembled for their approbation [approval];..." By a vote of 8 to 3, the words "for their approbation" were removed; there is nothing in the notes concerning any discussion about replacing the three words. Apparently, later the rest of the suggestion was removed. The wording to require Congress' approval of the Constitution was considered and was deliberately excluded by majority vote. If there was a common understanding that Congress had to approve the

Constitution, Mr. Dickinson would not have asked his question and the 8 to 3 vote would not have occurred without replacement language being discussed and eventually added. Also, if there was a common understanding that Congress had to approve the Constitution, the 8 to 3 vote ended the requirement. The absence of the requirement in Article VII was deliberate.

It should be noted that the first sentence in Article VI of the Constitution only applies to the federal government, per the current explanation provided by the U.S. Senate. Besides, the Constitution uses the words "the United States" in direct reference to the federal government while referring to the states as "the states." Arguably, the words "the United States" are used a few times in reference to a combined entity of the federal government and the states. Under this combined entity interpretation, the federal government and the states would not have been separate parties to the Articles of Confederation.

The Supreme Court's "political question" doctrine, which has no basis in the Constitution, prevents the Supreme Court from ruling that Congress shall call an Article V Convention that two-thirds of the state legislatures have properly applied for. Fortunately, consistent application of the Supreme Court's "political question" doctrine would prevent the federal government from interfering with the state legislature and the people's use of Article VII to restore the state legislatures' constitutional right to propose amendments, in a manner that this constitutional right can never again be blocked by the federal government. The Article VII Check and Balance (1) uses the political process of voting by the people, (2) is done the same way as the Constitution was ratified, (3) is a matter that the state legislatures and the people, just like for the Constitution, are the only segments of government involved, and (4) does not involve any judicial policymaking by the Supreme Court.

Our liberties need to be protected from people who profit by taking away our liberties. The Citizens Limit Congress Amendment protects our liberties by (1) restoring the constitutional check and balance on the federal government and (2) giving us a system that increases our control over how our money is spent.

We are way past the tipping point between the following:

 - the risk and consequence of what will happen when the financial-market revolt against our Treasury bonds ends up crashing both our economy and societal safety net

 - the risk and consequence of what will happen when the constitutional check and balance on the federal government is permanently restored and the people have a system that increases their control over how their money is spent

Article VII of our Constitution was written to allow as few as two-thirds of the states to ratify a new Constitution that would then go into effect for them, as well as go into effect for any other states that ratified it. This check and balance protects the Article V check and balance, which is being unconstitutionally blocked by the federal government. When the federal government, which was created by the Constitution, went into operation, two of the states had not ratified the Constitution. Establishment of the Constitution made the Articles of Confederation null and void for the states that ratified the Constitution. These states did not fulfill and did not need to fulfill the requirements in the Articles of Confederation for replacing, amending, and/or altering the Articles of Confederation.

When Congress proposes the Citizens Limit Congress Amendment, they will designate ratification by the state legislatures, in order to move things along as quickly as possible. Congress will not want to be responsible for any delays that could keep the people from preventing the crash of both the economy and societal safety net. Normally, money from Washington-special-interest groups gets split-up and used for misleading political advertisements that basically offset each other. If these groups worked together against ratification by the people, these groups' misleading political advertisements could sabotage the will of the people and would alienate Congress from the people and from the state legislatures.

The Constitutional Convention of 1787 only gave Congress ministerial duties. The Constitution was submitted/laid before Congress for consideration and then Congress was to submit it to the states for assent and ratification. It should be noted that no forms of the words "consideration" or "laid before" are used in the Constitution, Articles of Confederation, or the Declaration of Independence to intend a right to revise or a requirement of agreement before proceeding. Congress and George Washington's submittal letters with the Constitution to the states for ratification, made no reference to either of them agreeing with or approving the Constitution in any manner. There was no requirement for either of them to agree or approve the Constitution just like there was no requirement that the legislatures of all the states had to confirm the Constitution. When two-thirds of the states ratified the Constitution, it replaced the Articles of Confederation for these states, which made the entire Articles of Confederation null and void for these states.

The Constitution that the people ratified does not require Congress' approval of either the Constitution or any new Constitution that two-thirds or more of the states ratify. Even if the Constitution required Congress' approval of any new Constitution, which it does not, the requirement would become null and void, same as it was for the Articles of Confederation.

Even if Congress' approval was required back then, which it was not, it is not required now so no precedent from it back then would apply now; when something is no longer required, it cannot be said that it is still required based on it being done when it was required.

The Constitution excluded everything in the Articles of Confederation that could arguably block the state legislatures and the people from proposing and ratifying a new Constitution without Congress' permission. It went on to exclude Congress from any roll in ratifying the Constitution or in ratifying amendments to the Constitution. All three of these exclusions could not have been done by accident.

Article VII was not written based on the assumption that the requirements in the Articles of Confederation would be met; two-thirds of the states could have had their own new Constitution. Therefore, any requirement that Congress had to approve the Constitution would not have been left out of Article VII based on it being required by the Articles of Confederation. Even if it was, which it was not, there is nothing in effect now that requires Congress to approve any new Constitution that two-thirds of the states ratify.

Not requiring Congress' approval of any new Constitution is the most sensible/logical/expected thing to do. Why would the federal government have any veto power over the Constitution that created the federal government? Why would the states give up their power to change the Constitution that they wrote to create the federal government?

The federal government was intentionally excluded from having any way to block two-thirds of the states from having a new replacement Constitution. This was done to create a check and balance for times like now when the federal government abuses the Constitution. As soon as two-thirds of the state legislatures show their resolve to use the Article VII Check and Balance, the federal government will propose the Citizens Limit Congress Amendment, as written by the state legislatures.

In the highly unlikely event that Congress acts like a typical bully when its long-term victims try to free themselves, the states will prevail. Suppose the President issues an Executive Order or Congress rules that the Constitution requires Congress' approval of any Constitutional changes or any new Constitution, which it definitely does not. The answer to this is that just like two-thirds of the states could have had their own Constitution without meeting the requirements of the Articles of Confederation, two-thirds of the states can have their own new replacement Constitution now without meeting any requirements of the Constitution they replace. Congress could not block any new Constitution that two-thirds of the states ratify, just like the Continental Congress could not have blocked the new Constitution if only two-thirds of the states had ratified it.

Hopefully, our federal and state legislatures will think ahead to how all this will be recorded in the history books.

The Article VII Check and Balance is the fail-safe check and balance that the federal government cannot stop and the federal government will not force the states to use. This check and balance will remain an unused check and balance. The right to propose amendments will be permanently restored by the Citizens Limit Congress Amendment, in a manner that it cannot ever be blocked by the federal government again. The Citizens Limit Congress Amendment will be proposed by Congress and ratified by the state legislatures or by the people.

Ratifying a constitutional amendment that permanently restores the Constitution's check and balance on the federal government with changes to the check and balance so that it can never again be blocked by the federal government, does not create any sort of treaty, alliance, or confederation. The Constitution and the Articles of Confederation both forbid the states from entering into any of these three types of arrangements.

The part of Article VI of our Constitution about federal laws made in pursuance of the Constitution being the supreme law of the land is less restrictive on the states than what was in Article XIII of the Articles of Confederation, which was not an issue when our Constitution replaced the Articles of Confederation. Also, anything that the last 37 states to join the union could have originally agreed to when they joined the union would be less restrictive than what was in Article XIII of the Articles of Confederation. Even if it was not, a new Constitution creates a new federal government same as our current Constitution did.

Adding the Citizens Limit Congress Amendment is the only way to restore the Constitution's check and balance on the federal government with changes to the check and balance so that it can never again be blocked by the federal government. The people will not ratify the amendment, unless the people get their appropriate share of the power being transferred from Congress. There should be no reduction of the appropriate amount of power being transferred to the people, as contained in this book's Citizens Limit Congress Amendment draft.

When the state legislatures or people ratify the Citizens Limit Congress Amendment proposed in advance by Congress, the Article VII Check and

Balance will remain an unused check and balance and become much less likely to ever be needed.

There is nothing that is even close to being as dangerous to our Constitution as Congress crashing both our economy and societal safety net and then Congress "rebuilding" both our economy and societal safety net without any meaningful input from the state legislatures and the people. Congress will remain unable to stand up to the Washington-special-interest groups and will continue down the same path, increasing federal debt, increasing unfunded federal mandates, and building more inefficiencies into our economy. In addition, Congress will use the "national emergency," caused by the crash, to encroach further on our U.S. Constitutional Rights. Our standard of living will fall significantly relative to the rest of the world. Our societal safety net will probably never grow to the inflation-adjusted sustainable level it could have been maintained at.

It should be noted that it is very difficult to get citizens in each of any three-fourths of the states or state legislatures in each of any three-fourths of the states to ratify an amendment. Amendments proposed by citizens can be blocked by state legislatures in each of any 13 states. Amendments proposed by state legislatures can be blocked by majority vote of citizens in each of any 13 states.

Chapter 11

Citizens Limit Congress Amendment Draft

The preceding "Check and Balance on Congress" chapter explains the Constitutional basis for the states establishing the Citizens Limit Congress Amendment without any involvement by the federal government.

The Citizens Limit Congress Amendment has to be quickly ratified, one way or another, in 2021, to limit Congress and the Washington-special-interest groups from:

- crashing our economy and our societal safety net.

- "rebuilding" our economy and our societal safety net after they crash, without any meaningful input from the people and the state legislatures

- using the "national emergency" caused by the crash, to further reduce our constitutional rights

Citizens Limit Congress Amendment Draft, to be rewritten by the State Legislatures for Congress to propose as an Amendment:

Section 1. Any time from any place any two-thirds of the state legislatures can propose U.S. Constitutional Amendments. Ratification can only be done using the voting system in this amendment. Ratification of these proposed amendments will require a majority vote for the amendment by eligible citizens in each of any three-fourths of the states. State legislatures shall immediately promulgate ratified amendments they proposed. After all and only the above, these amendments shall become U.S. Constitutional Amendments that shall go into full effect for all the states and for the federal government immediately after promulgation. The federal government shall have no involvement with anything in this Section of the amendment, except the following. If the state legislatures do not immediately promulgate an amendment as above, Congress can promulgate it.

Section 2. Any time from any place eligible citizens can propose U.S. Constitutional Amendments by majority vote in each of any two-thirds of the states, using the voting system in this amendment. These proposed amendments can only be ratified by state legislatures in each of any three-fourths of the

states. State legislatures shall immediately promulgate ratified amendments they ratified. After all and only the above, these amendments shall become U.S. Constitutional Amendments that shall go into full effect for all the states and for the federal government immediately after promulgation. The federal government shall have no involvement with anything in this Section of the amendment, except the following. If the state legislatures do not immediately promulgate an amendment as above, Congress can promulgate it.

Section 3. This amendment's voting system shall enable 1% of eligible citizens in each of any five states to propose (1) federal cost reduction laws and (2) laws that redirect spending authorized by Congress, by submitting, within a 90-day period, the identically worded law to vote on. It will also enable voters to pass the laws within 60 days after being proposed. The laws can only be over-ruled by U.S. Constitutional Amendments. The percentage of states needed to each pass a federal cost reduction law by majority vote will be based on the percentage calculated as follows for the year two years earlier. For everyone who was at least 18 years old and living in the USA at the beginning of the year two years earlier, the federal government shall determine (1) the number of people who paid more in federal income taxes for that year than the federal government spent (directly or indirectly) on the person's living expenses and (2) the number of people who paid less in federal income taxes for that year than the federal government spent (directly or indirectly) on the person's living expenses. The number of people in the first group as a calculated percentage of all the people in both groups will be the required percentage of states that each need to pass any proposed federal cost reduction law by majority vote, except as follows. If the calculated percentage exceeds 75%, the federal cost reduction law's required percentage will be 75%. Living expenses include (along with other items) Medicaid, Medicare, Social Security, subsidized housing, subsidized medical insurance, college expenses, loans that do not have to be repaid, universal basic income, and cash assistance. The necessary government offices shall work together to develop the percentage. All details and assumptions need to be publically available, excluding social security numbers and names. Each person's details will be available on their voting portal, unless they opt-out. Administrative expenses can be identified to individuals based on each individual's receipts from the program being administered. Estimates used in the calculated percentage are acceptable as long as the calculated percentage is at the midpoint of the

99% confidence interval. The calculation needs to be audited by the GAO (General Accountability Office). Money spent for people's living expenses that cannot be tied to individual social security numbers, needs to be disclosed, detailed, and explained. Going forward, all federal and state expenditures for people's living expenses need to be broken out by recipients' social security number. Living expenses for dependent children that are paid to or for their parents, are considered living expenses of the parent. People who file their taxes as "married filing jointly", split the federal tax paid amount in half for each of their calculations. A federal cost reduction law is a law that reduces the total financial cost of federal laws upon the federal government, state governments, and U.S. citizens, without any of the reduced financial costs being used to increase financial costs elsewhere. Financial costs are all expenditures, loans made, loans guaranteed, increases in unfunded liabilities, and anything that increases debt now or in the future. If a federal cost reduction law ends up increasing the total financial costs, the law will become null and void. Questions concerning whether a federal cost reduction law will or does increase total financial costs, shall be answered within 30 days by the CBO (Congressional Budget Office) with a full explanation of how they determined their answer. The number of states needed to each pass a law that redirects spending authorized by Congress will be equal to three-fourths of the states.

Section 4. This amendment's voting system shall enable 50% of state legislatures to propose (1) federal cost reduction laws and (2) laws that redirect spending authorized by Congress. To pass a federal cost reduction law, the number of state legislatures needed to each pass it will be the same number of states with majority votes of citizens required to pass a federal cost reduction law in Section 3. To pass a law that redirects spending authorized by Congress, the number of state legislatures needed to each pass it will be the same number of states with majority votes of citizens required to pass a law that redirects spending authorized by Congress in Section 3. The laws in this Section can only be over-ruled by U.S. Constitutional Amendments, same as in Section 3.

Section 5. Within 28 days of a federal cost reduction law or a law that redirects spending or an amendment being proposed using this amendment's voting system, the CBO (Congressional Budget Office) will issue their forecast of the proposed law or amendment's effect on the federal debt and also on the state/local debt. Debt as use here includes everything that the federal government and the state/local governments are obligated to pay for, including things like agency debt and unfunded liabilities. The forecast will be for the first full year, and it will appear on the voting portal where people vote on the law or amendment. When the forecast is issued, the CBO web site will include all details, assumptions, and calculations used in the forecast and an explanation of how all the details, assumptions, and calculations were used.

Section 6. In states that do not allow all four things below, 1% of the eligible voters in the state can have a statewide vote using this amendment's voting system, where the majority of voters can require any or all of the following: (1) That this amendment's voting system be used for state elections. (2) That this amendment's voting system be used for state primaries. (3) That the run-off voting system in Section 7 be used whenever applicable. (4) That each political party, not already qualified to be on the ballot, can enter a person's name for each political position they are pursuing. Each name will then be on the ballot if at least 1% of eligible voters select the name on their voting portal prior to finalization of the ballot. These names will be on the ballot for each position, from the name selected the most, down to the name selected the least.

Section 7. When this amendment's voting system gets used for voting on anything where there are more than two choices and none get over 50% of the vote, a run-off vote will be held if allowed by state law. Choices will be included in the run-off voting based on which had the highest vote count, and will include just enough of these choices so that their combined vote count exceeded 50% of the vote. Additional run-off votes will be held if needed.

Section 8. This amendment's voting system must (1) keep everyone's vote secret, (2) allow everyone to verify if and how their vote was counted, (3) have the Social Security Administration and the state legislatures verify that every voter is an alive U.S. citizen who is old enough to vote, (4) have the U.S. Department of Justice verify that every voter has not been convicted of a federal crime or a crime in any state that would make the person ineligible to vote in their state, and (5) contain the following provision. Anyone convicted of violating a federal or state voting law in regards to voting in a this amendment's voting system, will receive a lifetime ban from having a federal job or working, directly or indirectly, under a federal contract.

Section 9. The Federal Government's Social Security Administration (SSA) will manage and have this amendment's voting system set up as described in this amendment. This voting system shall be used for all voting in this amendment.   Complete voting results will be broken out by state and included with each vote result. When a vote is entered in a voter's SSA portal, a sequential number is assigned, which gets recorded in both the portal (without being displayed) and along with the vote in the official tally of the votes. For a week after a voting period ends, eligible voters can go into their portal and see if and how their vote was counted in the official tally of votes. Anytime after voting, a voter can permanently block their portal from displaying the particular vote choice. No one can look up who voted and who did not vote. There will be a record of all transactions to and from each portal; this record will only be used if a person says that their vote was not counted correctly. Everyone who is eligible to vote can vote, even if they did not register to vote before the last day of the vote. Registering to vote requires the person to (1) enter information that the SSA already has, such as social security number and date of birth, and (2) update information the SSA has, such as primary home address and full legal name. Voters whose registration and/or eligibility determination are not completed before the vote, can cast their vote, which will be counted when the registration and eligibility determination are completed. This will delay the overall vote result for as long as the vote result would change if all and only the

remaining pending "No" votes were counted or
all and only the remaining pending "Yes" votes
were counted. When this amendment's voting
system is used by the people to vote for
candidates, the "No" and "Yes" above would be
replaced by all the candidate's names. Hacking
into someone else's voting portal will be a crime.
Casting someone else's vote without their
written permission and without entering, in the
portal, the name of the person casting the vote,
will be a crime. The SSA must give the states all
requested information the SSA has. The states
must give the SSA all requested information the
states have. Both the federal government and
the state legislatures shall independently verify
that only eligible U.S. Citizens vote in each of
this amendment's votes. The Federal Election
Commission can provide information that will
appear on the voting portal.

Section 10. Any federal government action after
2019 that the majority of voters in each of half
the states and/or half of the state legislatures
consider to be a reduction in their U.S.
Constitutional rights, shall be blocked from
being in effect until six months after the
following: Congress shall propose two U.S.
Constitutional Amendments, each of which just
reverses the action; one amendment shall be
designated for ratification by state legislatures
and the other shall be designated for ratification

by the people using this amendment's voting system.

Section 11. Using this amendment's voting system, a majority vote in each of more than any one half of the states can make changes concerning the frequency and timing of everything in this amendment.

Section 12. If this amendment is proposed by Congress, it's designated mode of ratification is by the state legislatures of any three-fourths of the states. There shall be no time limit for ratifying this amendment.

Section 13. Organizations can pay for and use this amendment's voting system to survey voters as follows: An organization can select anonymous survey participants based on which of this amendment's votes the voter voted in and/or did not vote in, as well as which voting district the voter is registered in. The organization can decide how much, if anything, each voter gets paid, by the voting system, for their response. The organization would just get anonymous survey results by voting district. Survey responses shall never be linked to the applicable voter.

Notes concerning the Citizens Limit Congress Amendment:

Each of the three entities, federal government, state legislatures, and the people will be subject to the other two entities proposing and ratifying U.S. Constitutional Amendments. In order for this to work properly in all three checks and balances, the entity that will be proposing the amendment must have total control over proposing the amendment, and the entity that will be ratifying the amendment must have total control over ratifying the amendment.

Section 1 of the Citizens Limit Congress Amendment restores the Constitution's check and balance on the federal government with changes to the check and balance so that it can never again be blocked by the federal government. Congress has unconstitutionally blocked the constitutional check and balance on the federal government by blocking the state legislatures from proposing amendments. See the "Congress Refuses to Call an Article V Convention" chapter in this book. State legislatures can never be able to ratify amendments they propose, because it would give them absolute control over the federal government and over the people. This amendment keeps the federal government from having any control over the ratification of amendments that are proposed using the Citizens Limit Congress Amendment. The following will not be in effect for amendments ratified using the Citizens Limit Congress Amendment: In Coleman v. Miller, the Supreme Court held that Congress had the final authority to determine the validity of an amendment's ratification.

Section 2 enables citizens to propose amendments that can only be ratified by state legislatures.

Section 3 sets up federal cost reduction laws and laws that redirect spending authorized by Congress, for citizens to propose and pass. These laws will not need to be proposed by Congress or by the state legislatures, but they can be over-ruled by an amendment. The Constitution's line between federal power and state/people power has been repeatedly crossed by the federal government; therefore, the people's federal cost reduction laws and laws that redirect spending authorized by Congress can cross the line the other way. The percentage of states required to each pass a federal cost reduction law, by majority vote, is perfectly matched to the problem it is designed to fix. The lower the percentage of people who pay more in federal income taxes than the federal government pays for their living expenses, the lower the percent of states required to pass a federal cost reduction law. If a minority of voters pay more in federal income taxes than they receive from the federal government for living expenses, this minority needs constitutional protection. The two-year delay after the year of the living expenses and taxes is necessary because final tax returns for a year can be routinely delayed until mid-October of the following year, and then the information needs to be processed. Voters need to know how generous their federal and state governments are, so they will be less likely to vote for candidates who promise to give them more from the government, but end up significantly reducing what they get from the government. Comparisons about income levels of rich people versus poor people, need three adjustments to properly measure the difference. Income needs to be after tax including Earned Income credit. The cost of government aid to people needs to be added to their income. Only citizens should be included in the results. Hopefully Congress provides ample warning about new and increased spending, so the state legislatures and people do not need to require the warning. Leaders, laws, and founding document changes for the European Union and for the U.S. Federal Government are not elected/passed by majority vote of all citizens; otherwise, less populous states would have been less likely to join their union. U.S. states were more like the European Union states, before Congress blocked the U.S. states' constitutional right to propose amendments.

Section 4 sets-up federal cost reduction laws and laws that redirect spending authorized by Congress, for state legislatures to propose and pass.

Section 5 is to get usable cost reduction information.

Section 6 can enable people to use the Citizens Limit Congress Amendment voting system for state elections, primaries, run-off voting, and to select candidates for their state ballot.

Section 7 would enable people to vote in the first round for the candidate that best represents them. This would increase ballot access for third parties like the Libertarian Party and the Green Party, for two reasons. First, higher vote counts for third parties in the first round will increase the chances that the third parties will have enough votes to automatically get ballot access in the future. Second, with the run-off voting system, state legislatures will have less of an objection to third parties getting on the ballot.

Section 8 is primarily about protecting the integrity of the people's voting in regard to proposing and ratify amendments.

Section 9 sets-up the Citizens Limit Congress Amendment voting system. The Citizens Limit Congress Amendment will be available for voting in primaries and elections, for states that use it that way. This will also provide a good way to test this system in parallel use with existing primary and election voting. Having the federal government administer the Citizens Limit Congress

Amendment voting system makes it easier for the people to monitor the voting versus having 50 states to monitor. Having both the federal government and the state legislatures independently verify that only eligible U.S. Citizens voted in each Citizens Limit Congress Amendment vote is critical, no matter who administers the Citizens Limit Congress Amendment voting. Voting on federal laws, for U.S. Constitutional Amendments, and for candidates is too important to have just one of these two parties do this verification. In the Athenian democracy, 2.5 millennium ago, people could only vote if both their parents were born in Athens.

Section 10 protects against the Supreme Court's "Political Question" doctrine being used in the future as an extension of the Supremacy Clause regarding the people and the state legislatures' constitutional rights. See the "Erosion of Constitutional Rights" chapter in this book.

Section 11 enables voters to use the Citizens Limit Congress Amendment voting system as efficiently as possible. When the state legislatures put together a version of the amendment that they agree on, they should adjust the frequency and timing of everything, as needed, so there is less for the voters to adjust.

Section 12 enables the federal government to simplify the ratification, rather than have

Washington-special-interest groups alienate the federal government from the people and from the state legislatures. It will demonstrate that there will be an effective check and balance on the people, same as the check and balance on the state legislatures and the check and balance on the federal government. All 27 U.S. Constitutional Amendments were ratified by state legislatures, except Amendment XXI, which repealed Amendment XVIII. Having no time limit for ratification is the best way to keep Washington-special-interest groups' money and influence from deciding whether an amendment gets added to our Constitution. Amendment XXVII was proposed in 1789 and ratified 202 years later in 1992. Also, Article VII has no time limit for ratification. Starting the Citizens Limit Congress Amendment's ratification process, with no time limit for ratification, will (1) immediately and always give Congress an incentive to significantly reduce federal government spending up until the time when the amendment is fully ratified, (2) immediately and always enable ratification to be quickly finalized after the crash of both our economy and societal safety net, and (3) immediately and always be in Congress' best interest to be more accommodating in its relationship with the people and the state legislatures.

Section 13 will create reliable survey results. The organization that pays for the survey can have the voting system certify any or all of (1) the selection criteria for all voters included in the survey, (2) the exact wording of everything the voters saw on their voting portal, and (3) the anonymous survey results that are all that the organization received.

State Legislators need to Live-Up to Alexander Hamilton's Expectation

When the people established their U.S. Federal Government, they also established the Article V and Article VII checks and balances. This enabled the people, working with their state legislatures, to always keep enough control to prevent Congress from doing anything significantly detrimental to our country, like crashing both our economy and societal safety net.

The Citizens Limit Congress Amendment will:

- enable people and state legislatures to reduce federal government spending

- enable people and state legislatures to redirect federal government spending, with a majority vote of people in each of any three-fourths of the states or by state legislatures in each of any three-fourths of the states, respectively

- enable people to propose U.S. Constitutional Amendments by a majority vote of people in each

of any two-thirds of the states that can be fully
ratified by state legislatures in each of any three-
fourths of the states

- enable state legislatures in each of any two-thirds
of the states to propose U.S. Constitutional
Amendments that can be fully ratified by a
majority vote of people in each of any three-fourths
of the states

- restore the Constitution's check and balance on
the federal government with changes to the check
and balance so that it can never again be blocked
by the federal government

- be the only way we have to limit Congress from
crashing then "rebuilding" our economy/societal
safety net and then using the "national emergency"
caused by the crash, to further reduce our
constitutional rights

Enabling people to propose amendments is
required to make sure that the people's ideas for
amendments are considered.

Enabling people and state legislatures to propose
amendments and ratify each other's proposed
amendments is critical to protect the people and
state legislatures' constitutional rights forever.

All of the above can be established by people and
state legislatures, the same way they established the
U.S. Constitution. Congress will make this
unnecessary by proposing the Citizens Limit

Congress Amendment that people and state legislatures get close to establishing without federal government involvement. By doing this, Congress will keep the Article VII Check and Balance unused and make it much less likely to ever be needed.

Article. VII. of the Constitution states - "The Ratification of the Conventions of nine States, shall be sufficient for the Establishment of this Constitution between the States so ratifying the Same."

The Constitution, with the addition of the states' Citizens Limit Congress Amendment and the other 27 amendments, just needs to be ratified by state conventions; the more state ratifications, the more accommodating that Congress will be.

Before ratification by two-thirds of the states, Congress will propose the states' Citizens Limit Congress Amendment for three-fourths of the states to ratify as an amendment. The Article VII Check and Balance will remain unused and it will become much less likely to be ever needed.

If the people in each of any two-thirds or more of the states did ratify the Constitution as above, it would <u>not</u> break the rules and agreements that maintain the perpetual union of the states. Instead, it would restore the state legislatures' constitutional right to propose amendments, in a manner that this constitutional right can never again be blocked by the federal government. Future historians would blame Congress for forcing the state legislatures and the people to use the Article VII Check and Balance to restore this constitutional right.

If the Article VII Check and Balance did get used as above, it would uphold the Constitution by (1) ratifying the Constitution and all existing amendments and (2) reusing Article VII to restore the state legislatures' constitutional right to propose amendments, in a manner that this constitutional right cannot ever be blocked by the federal government again. Congress is not upholding the Constitution when Congress refuses to call Article V Conventions that two-thirds of the state legislatures have properly applied for many times.

Congress cannot use the supremacy clause or anything else to block ratification by the people in each of any two-thirds of the states, just like the Continental Congress could not have used the first sentence in Article XIII of the Articles of Confederation or anything else to block the Constitution if only two-thirds of the states had ratified it.

When Article VII of the Constitution was written, the decision was made by an 8 to 3 vote to not require Congress' approval of the Constitution.

It should also be noted that (1) Congress was never asked to approve the Constitution, (2) Congress never approved the Constitution, and (3) Congress never said that they approved the Constitution.

The restriction in the Constitution on the states entering into a Treaty, Alliance, or Confederation with other states was also in the Articles of Confederation.

The first sentence of Article VI of the Constitution never applied to the states.

The Supreme Court's "political question" doctrine, which has no basis in the Constitution, prevents the Supreme Court from ruling that Congress shall call an Article V Convention that two-thirds of the state legislatures have properly applied for. Fortunately, consistent application of the Supreme Court's "political question" doctrine would prevent the federal government from interfering with the state legislature and the people's use of Article VII to restore the state legislatures' constitutional right to propose amendments, in a manner that this constitutional right can never again be blocked by the federal government. It (1) uses the political process of voting by the people, (2) is done the same way as the Constitution was ratified, (3) is a matter that the state legislatures and the people, just like for the Constitution, are the only segments of government involved, and (4) does not involve any judicial policymaking by the Supreme Court.

Our liberties need to be protected from people who profit by taking away our liberties. The Citizens Limit Congress Amendment protects our liberties by (1) restoring the constitutional check and balance on the federal government and (2) giving us a system that increases our control over how our money is spent.

We are way past the tipping point between the following:

- the risk and consequence of what will happen when the financial-market revolt against our Treasury bonds ends up crashing both our economy and societal safety net

- the risk and consequence of what will happen when the constitutional check and balance on the federal government is permanently restored and the people have a system that increases their control over how their money is spent

Article VII of our Constitution was written to allow as few as two-thirds of the states to ratify a new Constitution that would then go into effect for them, as well as go into effect for any other states that ratified it. This check and balance protects the Article V check and balance, which is being unconstitutionally blocked by the federal government. When the federal government, which was created by the Constitution, went into operation, two of the states had not ratified the Constitution. Establishment of the Constitution made the Articles of Confederation null and void for the states that ratified the Constitution. These states did not fulfill and did not need to fulfill the requirements in the Articles of Confederation for replacing, amending, and/or altering the Articles of Confederation.

When Congress proposes the Citizens Limit Congress Amendment, they will designate ratification by the state legislatures, in order to move things along as quickly as possible. Congress will not want to be responsible for any delays that could be blamed for keeping the people from preventing the crash of both the economy and societal safety net. Normally, money from Washington-special-interest groups gets split-up and used for misleading political advertisements that basically offset each other. If these groups worked together against ratification by the people, these groups' misleading political advertisements could sabotage the will of the people and would alienate Congress from the people and from the state legislatures.

Bipartisan support and cooperation will be required in the state legislatures to produce the states' version of the Citizens Limit Congress Amendment for Congress to propose. There should be no reduction of the appropriate amount of power being transferred to the people, as contained in this chapter's Citizens Limit Congress Amendment draft.

If the state legislatures do not work hard enough to establish the Citizens Limit Congress Amendment, they will end up being forever criticized by historians for letting Congress crash both our economy and our societal safety net.

When Congress crashes both our economy and our societal safety net, our state legislatures will need to quickly finish up establishing the Citizens Limit Congress Amendment. This will give the state legislatures and people meaningful input while Congress "rebuilds" our economy and our societal safety net. If our state legislatures do not protect us, we will need to ask ourselves the following questions. Are our state legislatures merely middle management that costs much more than its benefit to us? Have we reached the point where the federal government controls so much of what the state governments can and have to do, that now our Governors can just (1) oversee implementation of standardized federally mandated programs and policies and (2) handle the remaining things that the federal government currently allows the states to handle? After the crash, the states will most likely need to cut costs so that they can pay for the new unfunded mandates from Congress.

In The Federalist 85, where Alexander Hamilton reaffirms the state legislatures' right to propose amendments, he states, "We may safely rely on the disposition of the State legislatures to erect barriers against the encroachments of the national authority."

Since Article VII does not have a time limit for ratification, starting the Citizens Limit Congress Amendment ratification process will immediately and always give Congress an incentive to significantly reduce federal government spending up until the time when the state legislatures and the people can reduce federal government spending.

The different groups of state legislatures that want to propose different U.S. Constitutional Amendments, need to first work together. They need to restore the Constitution's check and balance on the federal government with changes to the check and balance so that it can never again be blocked by the federal government. Their current lack of much interest in amendments is because the state legislatures have submitted over 500 valid applications for an Article V Convention and Congress just refuses to call the convention.

These different groups of state legislatures cannot allow themselves to be split up into opposing groups, which is what will be attempted by the federal government, Washington-special-interest groups, and by some news media that advocate for centralized government.

The Citizens Limit Congress Amendment will have little effect on the current balance of power between Congressional Democrats and Congressional Republicans or between conservatives and liberals.

The problem today is Congress versus both the state legislatures and the people, not Congressional Republicans versus Congressional Democrats or Congressional Democrats versus Congressional Republicans. The problem is also not the poor versus the rich or the rich versus the poor, since crony capitalism and excessive entitlements make both these groups winners. The losers are the ordinary taxpayers and the states that have to pay for the debt and the unfunded mandates Congress creates to make those winners. Making those winners, also makes Congress a winner.

State legislatures have submitted the required number of valid applications for an Article V Convention many times, but Congress unconstitutionally refuses to call the convention. Even if an Article V Convention is called based on applications received in the past, would Congress (1) use its authority concerning "congressional promulgation" to block an amendment that is properly ratified by three-fourths or more of the states, (2) allow the proposing and ratifying to move quick enough to prevent Congress from crashing both our economy and societal safety net, (3) work with Washington-special-interest groups and some news media that advocate for a centralized government, to make the convention so disastrous that no one will want to discuss restoring the state legislatures' constitutional right to propose amendments for the next 50 years, (4) use the Supreme Court's "Political Question" doctrine to manipulate an Article V Convention into doing more harm than good, and (5) call future Article V Conventions that are applied for in accordance with Article V? Furthermore, would Congress engage in fear mongering concerning the unfounded possibility that the state legislatures proposing amendments could lead to a loss of personal freedoms, liberties, and equal rights. There is no such risk of this. All our personal freedoms, liberties, and equal rights come from the Constitution with Amendments, which were all ratified by the states. There is no way that three-fourths of the states would ratify an amendment that takes away our personal freedoms, liberties, or equal rights. The federal government has a long and extensive history of taking away our personal freedoms, liberties, and equal rights. I would rather trust my personal freedoms, liberties, and equal rights to a majority vote of people in each of any three-fourths of the states or to state legislatures in each of any three-fourths of the states, respectively.

Since the 2008 Financial Crisis, the federal debt has increased by more than $18 trillion. The effect of borrowing this $18 trillion made it seem like the 2008 Financial Crisis was no big deal. Repaying this $18 trillion, with interest, will have the opposite effect. Every time Congress kicks their debt problem farther down the road, the bigger the Federal Debt becomes and the bigger our inevitable crash will be.

When federal politicians state that the $2.8 trillion Social Security trust fund will cover Social Security checks for the next 15 to 20 years, they are leaving out a major detail. Congress borrowed the $2.8 trillion Social Security trust fund and spent it on non-Social Security programs that the Washington-special-interest groups wanted. Where is the $2.8 trillion going to come from to cover Social Security checks when Congress is already borrowing $1 trillion a year to fund non-Social Security programs? Also, where is the money to pay for the $10 trillion of Federal Agency Debt (Fannie Mae, Freddie Mac, Ginnie Mae, and Federal Home Loan Banks)? Medicare and Medicaid will also need future funding. The $28 trillion federal government debt is forecasted to grow by more than $1 trillion a year, even without any new spending programs.

Every year, in order to vote for raising the federal debt limit, which is required to keep the federal government from shutting down, Congress increases federal government spending by hundreds of billions of dollars without any real public debate. The federal debt limit does not reduce federal government spending, it just creates an excuse to increase federal government spending. Instead of approving each other's spending requests, the Congressional Republicans and Congressional Democrats should be fighting over how to spend the limited amount of money they are allowed to spend. For increasing the federal debt limit, there is no reason for Congress to spend more of our money.

When both our economy and societal safety net crash, Congress will not acknowledge any fault. Just like what happens now, Congressional Democrats will blame Congressional Republicans and Congressional Republicans will blame Congressional Democrats, all of which will distract people from realizing that the real problem is Congressional spending.

Proposing and ratifying the Citizens Limit Congress Amendment after Congress crashes both our economy and societal safety net will be difficult. The "national emergency" caused by the crash would delay and possibly prevent ratification of the Citizens Limit Congress Amendment. Even if the Citizens Limit Congress Amendment did get ratified after the crash, Congress and the Washington-special-interest groups will have new programs in effect that would be in the best interests of Congress and the Washington-special-interest groups. Most likely, these programs would be consuming all available money, and would be politically difficult to change without taking responsibility for their eventual failures.

Since Article VII does not have a time limit for ratification, starting the Citizens Limit Congress Amendment ratification process will immediately and always enable ratification to be quickly finalized after both the crash of our economy and our societal safety net. The state legislatures and the people will then have meaningful input when Congress and the Washington-special-interest groups "rebuild" both our crashed economy and our societal safety net.

The third immediate benefit of starting the Citizens Limit Congress Amendment ratification process, without any time limit, is that it will immediately and always be in Congress' best interest to be more accommodating in its relationship with the people and the state legislatures.

The more liberties the state legislatures and the people get, the more different ideas that different states will try concerning things like their school systems. The ideas that work well will spread to other states.

The business community has identified worldwide best practices used by businesses to improve efficiency. We need to identify worldwide best practices for government, so we can make sure our federal government uses our resources as efficiently as possible.

The liberties of the people are protected by the U.S. Constitution and its Amendments, which created the U.S. society we live in. Being a member of the U.S. society is why so many people around the world want to live in the U.S., even if they may never become U.S. citizens.

When the state legislatures lost their right to propose amendments, the people lost the power they had reserved for themselves in the Constitution. Now that the people are restoring the state legislatures' right to propose amendments, the people need the Citizens Limit Congress Amendment to permanently transfer the appropriate amount of power to the people.

The Citizens Limit Congress Amendment draft transfers the appropriate amount of power from Congress to the people, so that there will be an effective check and balance on the federal government. Congress will still be able to propose amendments and designate them for ratification by state legislatures or by the people.

There should be no reduction of the appropriate amount of power being transferred to the people, as contained in this chapter's Citizens Limit Congress Amendment draft.

When the state legislatures and the people can reduce and redirect federal government spending, the people and state legislatures will each be able to adjust where Congress and the Washington-special-interest groups make the required spending reductions.

Changing the income tax laws may seem to be an appealing alternative to reducing spending, but it would hardly make a dent in our debt and it could reduce tax revenues in the long-term. Wealth taxes reduce investment in our economy, which reduces employment, GDP, and taxable income. The wealth tax revenue would be more than offset by the reduced income tax revenue it causes. A consumption-based tax will tax the rich, without reducing investment in our economy. The greater the investment in our economy, the greater the economic opportunity for people who choose to work.

There is nothing that is even close to being as dangerous to our Constitution as Congress crashing both our economy and societal safety net and then Congress "rebuilding" both our economy and societal safety net without any meaningful input from the state legislatures and the people. Congress will remain unable to stand up to the Washington-special-interest groups and will continue down the same path, increasing federal debt, increasing unfunded federal mandates, and building more inefficiencies into our economy. In addition, Congress will use the "national emergency," caused by the crash, to encroach further on our U.S. Constitutional Rights. Our standard of living will fall significantly relative to the rest of the world. Our societal safety net will probably never grow to the inflation-adjusted sustainable level it could have been maintained at.

There is only one path that can save both our economy and our societal safety net from a devastating crash and keep our constitutional rights from slipping further. The path begins with the state legislatures working together and agreeing on a version of the Citizens Limit Congress Amendment for Congress to propose without any time limit for ratification, same as there is no time limit for ratification using Article VII.

State legislatures need to know that the people want the state legislatures to start working on the Citizens Limit Congress Amendment. Please contact both of your state legislators and ask them to start working on the Citizens Limit Congress Amendment as explained in this book.

The Citizens Limit Congress Amendment is just the mechanism that will appropriately split the power to create laws between the federal government, the state legislatures, and the people, with each being subject to a check and balance from the other two.

The Citizens Limit Congress Amendment is inevitable because it is the only workable solution to prevent Congress and the Washington-special-interest groups from (1) crashing both our economy and our societal safety net, (2) "rebuilding" both our economy and societal safety net without any meaningful input from the state legislatures and the people, and (3) encroaching further on the constitutional rights of the state legislatures and the people. The sooner the Citizens Limit Congress Amendment is established, the better.

Our state legislatures need to get working together and agree on a version of the Citizens Limit Congress Amendment for Congress to propose, before the state legislatures are blamed for letting the crash occur.

Enabling people and state legislatures to propose amendments and ratify each other's proposed amendments is critical for the following additional reason.

Our state legislatures and people need to be wary of false promises and Acts from Congress that will supposedly fix federal government spending. Back in the 1980s and 1990s people wanted Congress to balance the budget. Congress responded by passing a bunch of balanced budget type Acts. The people thought they had achieved their goal and moved on to other things. By the time that all these Acts failed to balance the budget, the people had nothing to hold Congress to its promises. Congress used the same scheme when people wanted campaign finance reform. The "Lock-Box" for social security positive cash flows is another example of false promises and Acts from Congress. Congress borrowed the money in the "Lock-Box" and spent it. Projections about when social security will run out of money are based on the "Lock-Box" money being used to pay social security benefits.

Chapter 12

Establishing the Check and Balance
On Congress

Congress' Federal Debt is now over $28 trillion and is growing by over $1 trillion a year. In addition, there is $10 trillion of Federal Agency Debt, $55 trillion of unfunded liabilities for Social Security and Medicare, and at least $12 trillion of unfunded liabilities for Medicaid. The larger the debt, the worse the crash will be. The crash will not be as bad as the 1929 Crash, but it will be much worse than the 2008 Crisis. The $38 trillion (Federal Debt plus Federal Agency Debt) of borrowed money is the amount that spending exceeded what our economy earned. Spending more than our economy earns, has to be eventually offset by spending less than our economy earns.

The reason why Democratic and Republican presidential candidates and congressional candidates did not seriously talk about reducing spending is because they are not planning to reduce spending.

The federal government cannot be allowed to continue unconstitutionally blocking the Constitution's check and balance on the federal government. See the "Congress Refuses to Call an Article V Convention" and the "Article V of the U.S. Constitution" chapters in this book.

Even if Congress calls an Article V Convention based on applications received in the past, there is not enough time to use the convention to stop Congress from crashing both our economy and our societal safety net. Even if there is enough time, the Supreme Court's "Political Question" doctrine would enable Congress to cause all kinds of problems with the Article V Convention.

The Citizens Limit Congress Amendment will:

- enable people and state legislatures to reduce federal government spending

- enable people and state legislatures to redirect federal government spending, with a majority vote of people in each of any three-fourths of the states or by state legislatures in each of any three-fourths of the states, respectively

- enable people to propose U.S. Constitutional Amendments by a majority vote of people in each of any two-thirds of the states that can be fully ratified by state legislatures in each of any three-fourths of the states

- enable state legislatures in each of any two-thirds of the states to propose U.S. Constitutional Amendments that can be fully ratified by a majority vote of people in each of any three-fourths of the states

- restore the Constitution's check and balance on the federal government with changes to the check and balance so that it can never again be blocked by the federal government

 - be the only way we have to limit Congress from crashing then "rebuilding" our economy/societal safety net and then using the "national emergency" caused by the crash, to further reduce our constitutional rights

Enabling people to propose amendments is required to make sure that the people's ideas for amendments are considered.

Enabling people and state legislatures to propose amendments and ratify each other's proposed amendments is critical to protect the people and state legislatures' constitutional rights forever.

All of the above can be established by people and state legislatures, the same way they established the U.S. Constitution. Congress will make this unnecessary by proposing the Citizens Limit Congress Amendment that people and state legislatures get close to establishing without federal government involvement. By doing this, Congress will keep the Article VII Check and Balance unused and make it much less likely to ever be needed.

Since Article VII of the U.S. Constitution does not have a time limit for ratification, the further the people and state legislatures go with establishing the Citizens Limit Congress Amendment by themselves:

 - the more that it will be in Congress' best interest to reduce federal government spending

 - the more that it will be in Congress' best interest to be accommodating in its relationship with the people and the state legislatures

 - the quicker that the people and state legislatures will have meaningful input in Washington after Congress crashes both our economy and our societal safety net

The different groups of state legislatures that want to propose different U.S. Constitutional Amendments, need to first work together. They need to restore the Constitution's check and balance on the federal government with changes to the check and balance so that it can never again be blocked by the federal government. Their current lack of much interest in amendments is because the state legislatures have submitted over 500 valid applications for an Article V Convention and Congress just refuses to call the convention.

These different groups of state legislatures cannot allow themselves to be split up into opposing groups, which is what will be attempted by the federal government, Washington-special-interest groups, and by some news media that advocate for centralized government.

When the state legislatures lost their right to propose amendments, the people lost the power they had reserved for themselves in the Constitution.

Bipartisan support and cooperation will be required in the state legislatures to produce the states' version of the Citizens Limit Congress Amendment for Congress to propose.

If the state legislatures do not work hard enough to establish the Citizens Limit Congress Amendment, they will end up being forever criticized by historians for letting Congress crash both our economy and our societal safety net.

When Congress crashes both our economy and our societal safety net, our state legislatures will need to quickly finish up establishing the Citizens Limit Congress Amendment. This will give the state legislatures and people meaningful input while Congress "rebuilds" our economy and our societal safety net. If our state legislatures do not protect us, we will need to ask ourselves the following questions. Are our state legislatures merely middle management that costs much more than its benefit to us? Have we reached the point where the federal government controls so much of what the state governments can and have to do, that now our Governors can just (1) oversee implementation of standardized federally mandated programs and policies and (2) handle the remaining things that the federal government currently allows the states to handle? After the crash, the states will most likely need to drastically cut costs so that they can pay for the new unfunded mandates from Congress.

In The Federalist 85, where Alexander Hamilton reaffirms the state legislatures' right to propose amendments, he states, "We may safely rely on the disposition of the State legislatures to erect barriers against the encroachments of the national authority."

There is only one path that can save both our economy and our societal safety net from a devastating crash and keep our constitutional rights from slipping further. The path begins with the state legislatures working together and agreeing on a version of the Citizens Limit Congress Amendment for Congress to propose without any time limit for ratification, same as there is no time limit for ratification using Article VII.

State legislatures need to know that the people want the state legislatures to start working on the

Citizens Limit Congress Amendment. Please contact both of your state legislators and ask them to start working on the Citizens Limit Congress Amendment as explained in this book.

The Citizens Limit Congress Amendment is just the mechanism that restores having the people, state legislatures, and the federal government each be subject to a check and balance from the other two.

The Citizens Limit Congress Amendment is inevitable because it is the only workable solution to prevent Congress and the Washington-special-interest groups from (1) crashing both our economy and our societal safety net, (2) "rebuilding" both our economy and societal safety net without any meaningful input from the state legislatures and the people, and (3) encroaching further on the constitutional rights of the state legislatures and the people. The sooner the Citizens Limit Congress Amendment is established, the better.

Made in the USA
Middletown, DE
28 February 2021